GERARD CHRISPIN

# Beyond Bars

## Looking inside the inside story

DayOne

© Day One Publications 2007
First printed 2007

ISBN 978–1–84625–094–1

Unless otherwise indicated, Scripture quotations are from the **New King James Version (NKJV)®**. Copyright © 1982 by Thomas Nelson, Inc. Used by permission. All rights reserved.

British Library Cataloguing in Publication Data available

Published by Day One Publications
Ryelands Road, Leominster, HR6 8NZ
☎ 01568 613 740 FAX 01568 611 473
email—sales@dayone.co.uk
web site—www.dayone.co.uk
North America—e-mail—usasales@dayone.co.uk

Cover design by Bradley Goodwin
Printed by Gutenberg Press, Malta

*In a unique way, Gerard Chrispin skilfully uses down-to-earth, up-to-date language to retell familiar Bible stories, then synchronizes them with modern case histories. The result is twofold: one is clearly reminded that there are no 'new sins', only the old ones in modern dress, and that not even the deepest-dyed sinners are beyond the reach of God's sovereign grace.*

**—John Blanchard, internationally known Author, Evangelist, Conference Teacher and Apologist**

# Dedication

*To Phillippa*

with all my love.

Thank you for the 'life sentence' for which I thank God.

I am so glad that I did not miss it!

# Contents

# Glossary of terms

**ABH** —assault occasioning actual bodily harm

**Archbold** —a much used and respected criminal law practice textbook

**ASBO** —anti-social behaviour order

**Banged-up**—imprisoned, or more specifically locked in your cell

**Bird, or doing bird**
—doing time in prison

**Blackstone**—a much used and respected criminal law practice textbook

**Bottle** —courage (He's got no bottle = he dare not do it)

**Cat A, Cat B, Cat C, Cat D**
—categories of prison security from A (strict) to D (open).

**Category A, Category B, Category C, Category D**
—as above

**Cons** —convictions, also convicts

**CRO** —criminal record

**GBH** —assault occasioning grievous bodily harm

**Grass** —informer

**Grassed, or grassed up**
—having been reported or informed against

**HMP** —Her Majesty's Prison

**ID** —identification

**Lifer** —a prisoner serving a life sentence, mainly for murder

**Listener** —a prisoner officially asked to spend time listening to other prisoners' problems

**Nick** —prison

**Nicked** —arrested

**PACE** —Police and Criminal Evidence Act

**PMA** —Prison Ministry Associate of DAYLIGHT Christian Prison Trust

**PMV** —Prison Ministry Visitor of DAYLIGHT Christian Prison Trust

**PO** —a prison officer who is a Principal Officer

**Precons** —previous convictions

**Recidivism** —reoffending

**RD** —Regional Director of DAYLIGHT Christian Prison Trust

**Screw** —prisoners' slang for prison officer

**Seg** —Segregation Unit of a prison, where controlled solitary confinement takes place

**Shooter** —a gun

**SO** —a prison officer who is a Senior Officer

**Stitched up**
    —framed or set up to fail

**Stones** —Stones Justices' manual, a criminal law textbook used in Magistrates' Courts

**VP** —vulnerable prisoner

**YOI** —Young Offenders' Institution

The Letter to the Hebrews comes towards its end with what James Moffatt once called 'a handful of moral counsels'. One of these seems at first reading to be nothing more than a special prayer request—'Remember those who are in prison, as though in prison with them' (Hebrews 13:3)—but it may have been much more than that, as earlier in the letter the writer commends the readers for having 'had compassion on those in prison' (Hebrews 10:34). I am struggling to remember when I last heard anybody pray for prisoners, while having practical compassion on them seems to have few takers. Yet this 'blind spot' is totally at odds with the robust Christianity we see on the pages of the New Testament, something recognized by Jesus himself when he commended prison visiting with the words, 'I was in prison and you came to me' (Matthew 25:36).

As a pagan orator once noted, the early Christians' loving, practical compassion for those of their number incarcerated for their faith was proverbial: 'If they hear that any one of their number is in prison or in distress for the sake of their Christ's name, they all render aid in his necessity and, if they can, they redeem him, to set him free.' There are even instances when Christians sold themselves into slavery to raise the necessary funds to free a fellow believer.

Over the centuries there have been stirring examples of the way in which believers have demonstrated their commitment to Christ by their concern for those behind bars, and countless thousands of prisoners who have never heard of her have cause to be grateful for the work of Elizabeth Fry (1780–1845) who pioneered prison reform in Britain and Europe, sponsored work among London's homeless, and formed a society for the care and rehabilitation of discharged criminals.

Attending a futile bail application, Gerard Chrispin heard the Chairman of the Magistrates' bench describe the prisoner concerned as 'a waste of space'. That throwaway phrase made such an impact on Gerard that soon afterwards he gladly accepted an invitation to become involved in full-time (and front line) prison ministry. Drawing on his first few years in this challenging work, *Beyond bars* is by way of being a report of 'work in progress': it is also a much-needed wake-up call to the Christian church.

Although my visiting of prisons began over forty years ago, when I served as Secretary to the States of Guernsey Prison Board, my own opportunities to take the gospel behind prison walls have been few and far between. Here, by contrast, we are guided by someone familiar on an ongoing basis with life 'inside'. It is a real eye-opener, giving glimpses of robbers and rapists, murderers and violent thugs, as well as illegal immigrants and others guilty of 'white collar crimes'.

In a unique way, Gerard Chrispin skilfully uses down-to-earth, up-to-date language to retell familiar Bible stories, then synchronizes them with modern case histories. The result is twofold: one is clearly reminded that there are no 'new sins', only the old ones in modern dress, and that not even the deepest-dyed sinners are beyond the reach of God's sovereign grace. It is encouraging to know that 98% of prisoners who are offered Christian literature are glad to accept it and it is thrilling to read of hardened criminals, thrown into the state's 'rubbish tip', listening attentively to clear gospel presentations, and of some prisoners being transformed by the power of the gospel and going on to lead reformed lives that demonstrate the biblical truth that 'if anyone is in Christ, he is a new creation. The old has passed away; behold, the new has come' (2 Corinthians 5:17).

At one point the author asks, 'How involved is the Christian church in prison and prisoners? Do most Christians see it as an arena of need or as a spectacle to watch from afar? How much of the resources of time, money and effort are channelled into this needy mission field by individual believers and by Christian churches?' The story of DAYLIGHT Christian Prison Trust, arising out of Day One Prison Ministries, points to ways in which many could respond to the challenge. May God graciously grant that this will happen!

**John Blanchard,**
Internationally known Author, Evangelist, Conference Teacher and Apologist

L et me start with a huge 'THANK YOU' to all who further the Lord's work in prisons by praying for, giving to, helping with, and going to prison for DAYLIGHT Christian Prison Trust, or who support its associate, Day One Prison Ministries. Also an equally big vote of thanks to the many HMP Chaplains in the UK's 160 plus prisons who kindly invite DAYLIGHT to take services, meetings and Bible studies in their prisons and who enable us to meet pastorally 'one-on-one' with certain inmates. I will complete my words of thanks later in this Preface .

The first ten chapters of *Beyond bars* are made up of five chapters adapted and expanded from original magazine articles, and five new chapters, though not in that order.

The longer Chapter 11 unfolds the development of the current work from the start. Starting with the formation of Day One Prison Ministries (with which DAYLIGHT continues to work in close association), it traces DAYLIGHT Christian Prison Trust's creation and early development from that early vision. This aspect of the prison story is told from my personal viewpoint. I hope that Chapter 12, the final chapter, builds on that and will provoke some thought, prayer and action.

Appendix One carries some letters from prisoners, augmenting those in Chapter 8. Appendix Two contains DAYLIGHT's basis of belief. It is important both to *hold* and to *communicate* Biblical truth.

To avoid identifying inmates, I have changed their names and some surrounding personal details and circumstances. It would be wrong to betray confidences or for them to risk recognition. I have used some poetic licence to flesh out some biblical situations. No truths or principles of Scripture have been compromised thereby. To say more now might spoil the plot! Bible passages at the end of each chapter are best read *after* the chapter itself, for the same reason!

I would like to stress two points before you read the book, please.

First, we have not seen many converts yet. I do not believe that the cause of Christ is helped by reports of blessing and revival that stretch honesty to the limit and beyond. I recently read about how David Brainerd was on the point of giving in his notice as a missionary to the North American Indians because of so little fruit, when unexpectedly (and not very dramatically, but very really) revival took place and sinners were saved and changed. At times I have felt like he did, but reminded myself that the regular attentive listening to the gospel by men and women outside Christ *must* yield fruit when God's Holy Spirit works on their lives. That fruit might come through others or even after I am in glory. *But all the same, I yearn for real converts*, and we have not seen many yet that we know about from our work. I am grateful to God that we have seen Him at work in some, however. What a joy recently to be told by a previously violent young offender that 'I could not stop praying even as I brushed my teeth!' He then recounted how he had turned down two challenges for fights simply because he had trusted Christ.

Second, please never underestimate the difficulty in following up people when they leave prison, or in their carrying on with the Lord when they are released. How we need to see God's 'amazing grace' at work time and again!

I do not raise these two points to discourage my readers but to remind them that there is a spiritual battle here. May I ask those who know Christ to turn issues into prayer for blessing and for God's glory as they read, please? To any reading this book who have not yet personally come to know Jesus Christ as your Lord and Saviour my prayer is that through it God will help you to do just that.

I have a number of people I want to thank specifically for their help, either in the work, or in publishing the book, or in both. I am absolutely sure that none of them would ask for thanks from me, but I can do nothing else.

Once more, I say 'thank you' to my good friend David Harding, who again edited internally a book by me before I unleashed it on the publisher. David is one of my very first ports of call whenever I need good biblically applied common sense (very rare today!), a second opinion, or to check that I am not just about to become a heretic.

I am also greatly obliged to John Blanchard for kindly reading the book and providing the foreword for it. I do not know how he makes the time to do that in all his busy, prolific and fruitful speaking and writing ministries. He amazes me—but that is God's grace at work.

I am also indebted to Huw Kinsey of the Evangelical Movement of Wales (EMW), who first asked me to write five articles for EMW's excellent magazine 'The Evangelical'. I am grateful to EMW for their ready permission and encouragement to me now to include them, albeit modified and expanded, in this book. Day One Publications had already commissioned a book on prison from me. Without including these revised articles written for 'The Evangelical', this book might still have been on my growing 'action' list!

I am grateful to another good friend and former Day One colleague, Jim Holmes, and to his capable and professional Day One team for their customary but crucial help and skill in producing this book.

Thank you to John Roberts for his initial vision which led to Day One's donation of very many Day One diaries each year to HMP chaplains to give to inmates and to some staff. This led to the formation of the frontline gospel work of Day One Prison Ministries, which I was privileged to pioneer and direct for seven years. When Day One later decided to concentrate its future prison input into the ongoing generous provision of those diaries for prisoners, my colleagues and I were strongly encouraged by John to develop and expand the frontline work 'beyond bars' through DAYLIGHT Christian Prison Trust, still in close association with Day One. Day One Prison Ministries now operates independently and still donates those magnificent little diaries, and DAYLIGHT helps to organise the diary distribution as part of that valued association.

Thank you also to my many willing colleagues in DAYLIGHT Christian Prison Trust. Without the initial encouragement—by his fellowship, friendship and hard work—of Paul Philpott, the Chairman of DAYLIGHT's trustees and Coordinator of our Prison Ministry Associates and Prison Ministry Visitors, DAYLIGHT would never have got off the ground. Lyndon Day, as our administrator and accountant, works long, hard and very effectively to keep the work friendly and efficient. By so doing, he enables us all to spend more valuable time at 'the coal face' than otherwise could be the case. My admiration for his generous service, cheerful willingness, and work ethic goes with my deep thanks.

I must also express my gratitude to our team of dedicated, involved and concerned trustees and to our valued Council of Reference of godly leaders and ministers who have so kindly lent their names and prayers to the work.

The trouble with making a 'thank you' list is, sadly, that people get missed unintentionally. Nevertheless, thank you to Ruth French, Nigel Murray, Hilda Sayers, and Simon Young for their regular sacrifice of time and effort in, respectively, publicity, producing and distributing evangelistic CDs, secretarial help, and IT matters.

DAYLIGHT's band of Prison Ministry Associates and Prison Ministry Visitors, who carry on the vital gospel work in their more local prisons on an honorary basis, along with our (hopefully growing) salaried staff of Regional Directors, are the life blood of the future of this work. They go to preach and teach and seek to involve other Christians and churches. They will already know the blessings from the Lord of the harvest for this service for Him, as will the churches and fellowships who are involved or who seek to be involved with us in seeking prisoners for Christ. But I add my thanks, nevertheless.

My last 'thank you' is to Phillippa. She is much more than my wife and best friend. Ever cheerful and tireless in organising our schedules to prisons, developing our valued friendships with prison chaplains, following up inmates, arranging promotional visits to churches and fellowships, and coming with me to prison after prison to share Christ with inmates, she is a constant calming influence on her sometimes not very spiritual husband through her wise and gracious advice and support. Already we have had 'downs' in the work as well as 'ups' and she is a constant help and encouragement. I love her and thank her. She will tell me off when she finds that I have written this here!

I hope this book gives some insight into prison, reaching prisoners with the gospel and helping them, and the need for other Christians to be involved. If this encourages Christians to pray for, join in or support prison gospel work, I shall be delighted. If that includes their involvement in DAYLIGHT Christian Prison Trust, whose work I earnestly pray will continue to be blessed in the future long after I have ceased to be its General Director, I shall be even more delighted. If it helps other readers to come to know the Lord, I shall be more thrilled than I can possibly say!

**Gerard Chrispin**
DAYLIGHT CPT, P O Box 3173, Swindon, SN6 7WN
Email: Prison@DaylightCPT.org Internet www.DaylightCPT.org

# 'Lock the cell door and throw away the key!' Really?

## Two men who had gone too far into crime ever to change. Or had they?

### Tommy—the armed drug dealer

He showed me the photographs and reports in the newspaper cuttings. I could understand why his rugged and once good-looking face today looks like a scarred, cut and stitched up football. That all came in the early hours of the morning on a city street where Tommy had been worked over thoroughly by a violent gang with iron bars and baseball bats. Bleeding, battered and unrecognisable, he had been left for dead. His large, square and extremely muscular frame made me realise why it would have needed at least four or five strong-willed and strong-armed thugs to silence Tommy. He was a particularly powerful man, a street fighter as well as a schemer, and an extremely nasty and vicious armed drugs dealer. When he double-crossed the gang he worked with, he proved by painful and life-threatening experience that he was by no means the only man to match that frightening description.

Murderers are instantly recognisable as being on the outside edge of unacceptable criminality. Even with the justified public outcry against the growing cancer of paedophile offences and vicious rapes, murder (including terrorist mass murder of innocent unsuspecting victims) would probably still be voted the worst crime on a public opinion poll. It is so final. Have you ever considered that drug dealers like Tommy are potentially some of the worst kind of murderer? Many regard people like him as even more culpable than the violent thug or person who wrongly responds by killing someone in the heat of passion, or as a mistake when he intended to give his victim a good hiding. Drug dealers coldly calculate ('calculate' is the right word because they do it for financial gain) their evil activities, knowing that they will destroy and decimate the lives of many. They will cause the accelerating death of many hopeless and desperate addicts just as certainly as a man using a gun, knife or poison. And who knows how many secondary victims are broken and discarded in their criminal 'genealogy' as those addicts also assault, rob and kill others to feed their habits? How many heartbroken mothers, fathers, children, brothers, sisters and other family members and friends sob bitterly in the wake of the drug dealers' insatiable greed for money, no matter what harm they cause others?

## Double-whammy

Tommy suffered a huge double-whammy. Not only did the vengeful and terrifying violent gang that he double-crossed catch up with him and beat him to pulp, breaking many bones in his immensely strong body, but through their intervention the police found, crumpled in the street in a pool of blood, the shattered wreck of the man they had long since been looking for. They thought they had found a corpse, but Tommy's iron resolve and courage (often misplaced before) was no less than his legendary physical strength. Tommy would never lose anything without a fight. He did not die. After initial extensive emergency surgery had enabled him to pull though, and after identification was possible, his recovery began in a prison hospital with later recuperation taking place in a series of lonely prison cells in a Category A prison.

## Presence

Even now, Tommy really did look frightening. When he simply came to sit down and listen to the gospel being shared at an extended meeting one afternoon, in the prison where he was nearing the end of his sentence, he brought 'presence' into the room. I found it hard not to look at him to gain his tacit approval for what I was saying! Had I not been preaching God's word and sharing the gospel of the almighty Lord of the universe, I might have yielded to that temptation. But in any case I need not have worried! Tommy was clearly 'on my side'.

## True for the inmate with the longest 'CRO'

In that crowded prison chapel room, I shared with the forty prisoners the amazing news that Christ died for our sins upon the cross, bearing in His holy and sinless body the punishment that we deserve for that wrongdoing. I assured them that Jesus had risen from the dead and was alive. Any person who would really turn his back on his sins in repentance and trust Christ personally could know God's forgiveness, a new life in Him, and the certainty of heaven to come. That was as true for the inmate with the longest 'CRO' (the accepted abbreviation for 'criminal record') as it was for the nicest unconverted churchgoing hypocrite.

## Question Time

A lively, serious and detailed question time followed next. It made David Dimbleby's *Question Time* on BBC TV look like a playgroup in a sunny meadow! I sought to answer the prisoners' questions as logically, clearly and compellingly as I could straight from the Bible, straight from the heart and straight from the shoulder. They are not interested in calling a spade an 'agricultural implement'! I was pleased to see nods of agreement and some expressions indicating that at least some light was dawning. However, as with Paul at Mars Hill in Acts 17, some were unconvinced, while the faces of others had doubt written on them. God can save people the first time they hear the gospel, but it usually takes a lot longer.

## Enter Tommy, the preacher!

That's when Tommy struck up in his distinctive local accent—far more effectively than I had done. I don't know how one man could 'eyeball' forty mainly rough inmates at the same time, especially when he was sat with them—but he did! Like an Italian 'godfather', he looked around at (or perhaps through!) his fellow offenders with a burning intent and transparent sincerity that compelled each one to listen and to show that *he* was listening.

'You all know me,' he reminded them, 'and I'm telling you straight that what the preacher said is dead right. OK?' Nearly all nodded in approval as his gaze met them! Perhaps doubt and denial were still in the minds of some, but they were not going to show it at that precise moment!

As he spoke, Phillippa and I noticed the big Bible he was holding. Rather like his face, it was extremely worn and battered. It was obviously very well read and often thumbed. If someone's Bible is in tatters, their life is probably not!

## Stopped in his tracks in his cell

Tommy went on to describe his past life in detail, which would not shock the men in that room nearly as much as it would a Sunday congregation. Without in the least condoning or glorifying his life of violence, greed, immorality and selfish pleasure, he talked in down-to-earth (but by no means crude) untheological terms of the depth of his need for forgiveness and of the amazing new life he had found in Christ. God had stopped him in his tracks in his cell. After contact with a local visiting Christian, he confessed his sins to God and turned to Him in faith, realising that Jesus had died for him. Now the Bible had come to life and he prayed every day because he wanted to. Christ had changed him.

## No one argued!

He looked around again and said, 'You all know that this is true, because you all know me.' No one argued! Later I found that, while he was regarded by some as an 'extremist' (though I don't think they mentioned it to Tommy!), everyone who knew him before had to accept that he was different. He still could lose his temper, but not at all like he used to, and now never with violence or the threat of it. Also apologies came sincerely and voluntarily if he did lose his cool. No one thought he was perfect, but they accepted that God was real to him. In fact he was allowed to counsel men because the authorities saw his excellent influence on them.

How very sad it would have been if he had been murdered in that street. How inappropriate to have said, 'Lock the cell door and throw away the key.' Yet some would have taken that view based on his wicked personal history.

## Just one concern

I met him several times again and heard from him after his release. Even with some changed facts to hide his true identity, you can see that Tommy is a real trophy of God's saving grace! I was concerned, however, that some well-meaning and commendably supportive Christian folks might put him on a public platform very soon after he came out of prison. I had advised him to keep a low profile for a period and first prove his repentance and conversion by his changed life over an observable period of time. Young

Christians with a riveting criminal past to relate can too easily attract an undiscerning (even Christian) audience. They can fall into pride and lose their humble reliance on the Lord. That can be as true for an 'ex con' who is well educated or a celebrity as it can for men like Tommy. Surely the biblical principle of 1 Timothy 3:6, applying in context to church leadership, also has a wider application here?

## Manny—'the scum'

Manny was very, very different—or was he? Unlike Tommy, he had been brought up by a God-fearing and very influential and wealthy father. (I don't think Tommy ever knew who his dad was.) Manny was raised to do what was right, to seek to worship and please God, and to admit he was wrong when he was wrong. However, even by the age of twelve, he rebelled strongly and viciously against his godly background. Seldom could there have been such a sad and complete contrast between a godly father and his wicked son. He did not rebel against God and His standards in ignorance—God spoke strongly to his conscience but he would not listen. A seared conscience is a potential springboard for all kinds of evil. That is why the Christian must keep it tender before God.

## Manny's evil deeds

Manny's excesses included devil-worship, immersion in the occult, fortune-telling, idolatry and he was even part of a satanic circle that abused and killed children in the name of the vile religion he promoted. He also desecrated true places of worship and influenced many others to do evil. He led many thousands of people astray into rank wickedness.

Today the only place for men and women like Manny in prison in the UK would be the 'VPU' (vulnerable prisoners' unit). He would be torn limb-from-limb if the 'normal' prisoners could get hold of him. Many of the other inmates call VPs 'the scum', even though some are not there because of paedophile offences or sexual abuse. (About a third of them are suicidal or self-harmers, or especially vulnerable to bullying, or former policemen or judges, or else in minority groups that attract the violence of other prisoners.) But Manny was exactly the type of detested and hated VP who would not have got out of a normal prison wing alive, if ever it was considered safe to release him. Perhaps the Moors murder cases are the nearest I can think to compare with that aspect of his situation. (Those infamous cases concerned the sadistic torture and murder of children, whose bodies were buried in the Pennines in the rugged north of England.) But Manny was far worse than the two people convicted in those cases— Myra Hindley and Ian Brady—put together. Even now, I think that a large part of our fellow citizens facing a 'Manny situation' in our country today would ask for the death sentence to be reintroduced, or shout 'Lock the cell door and throw away the key!'

## Through affliction in prison to faith in God

But Manny was in custody in a non-UK prison a long time ago, and without any inbuilt protections from current law. He suffered greatly and was subjected to intense physical pain and humiliation there. He was fettered and had a hook put through his nose. This was done to treat him like a captured animal, and make him look like one, too. Yet he survived and in that affliction in custody—in fact because of it—he humbled himself before God and prayed to Him. In that prayer he turned to God from his sin in principle, and from the many sins he had committed. Like Tommy, he, too, came personally to know God and His life-changing mercy and grace.

God not only forgave his sins and changed him from the inside out, but He intervened to deliver him from the inside of prison to outside freedom also.

Such was the difference in his life and the change in his new-found integrity that King Manasseh of Judah (for that is who 'Manny' was) removed the hideous idolatry he had embraced, turned his back on witchcraft and the occult, reversed the vile and cruel practices which he had promoted, and became a man of integrity and compassion, returning to worshipping the only God who could forgive him. He also ruled better as a king. No more would innocent victims die as a result of the cruelty previously spawned by his callous rejection of God's word in following false and wicked religious practices.

As you can see from 2 Chronicles 32:32–33 and 33:1–20 (copied at the end of this chapter), this son of good King Hezekiah proved that God will forgive and change the worst of sinners, through genuine repentance and personal faith in Him. A life renewed in this way can become truly influential for Him. Can a person commit such great evil or so many sins that they are beyond God's grace and mercy? Manasseh proves that no one has gone 'too far' who is willing to turn and trust our merciful Saviour God: not VPs, not murderers, and not even Manny.

## Throw away the prejudice—not the key!

It would have been as sad for Manasseh as for Tommy, and a lot worse for the nation he influenced for God as a result of his conversion, if someone had locked the cell door and thrown away the key. Such thinking ignores the power, mercy and grace of God.

That is not a comment on the issue of the rightness or wrongness of capital punishment for murder, because it could be equally argued that facing the death penalty might make a convicted murderer square up to reality, realise eternity was near, and turn to Christ. Dr Johnson said that a man's knowledge that he was about to be executed for his crime 'concentrated his thinking wonderfully.' (Anyhow, I am not addressing capital punishment in this book.) Rather we must bear in mind that no living sinner is beyond the reach of God and the gospel of His Son who 'bore our sins in His body on the tree' (1 Peter 2:24). We should seek to pray for and reach with the gospel the worst of men and women, inside or outside prison.

It is far better and God-honouring to throw away our prejudices, pray that prisoners will repent and be converted, and that—where possible (and sadly it is sometimes too late)—they approach victims humbly for their forgiveness and do what they can to express and evidence their sorrow over their sin. Pray that those who have offended our holy God and hurt others will yet live to be a blessing to others who otherwise might have been among their next victims.

**NOW READ WHAT THE BIBLE SAYS IN 2 CHRONICLES 32:32–33 AND 33:1–20:**

2 Chronicles 32:

32 Now the rest of the acts of Hezekiah, and his goodness, indeed they are written in the vision of Isaiah the prophet, the son of Amoz, and in the book of the kings of Judah and Israel. 33 So Hezekiah rested with his fathers, and they buried him in the upper tombs of the sons of David; and all Judah and the inhabitants of Jerusalem honoured him at his death. Then Manasseh his son reigned in his place.

2 Chronicles 33:

1 Manasseh was twelve years old when he became king, and he reigned fifty-five years in Jerusalem. 2 But he did evil in the sight of the LORD, according to the abominations of the nations whom the LORD had cast out before the children of Israel. 3 For he rebuilt the high places which Hezekiah his father had broken down; he raised up altars for the Baals, and made wooden images; and he worshiped all the host of heaven and served them. 4 He also built altars in the house of the LORD, of which the LORD had said, 'In Jerusalem shall My name be forever.' 5 And he built altars for all the host of heaven in the two courts of the house of the LORD. 6 Also he caused his sons to pass through the fire in the Valley of the Son of Hinnom; he practiced soothsaying, used witchcraft and sorcery, and consulted mediums and spiritists. He did much evil in the sight of the LORD, to provoke Him to anger. 7 He even set a carved image, the idol which he had made, in the house of God, of which God had said to David and to Solomon his son, "In this house and in Jerusalem, which I have chosen out of all the tribes of Israel, I will put My name forever; 8 and I will not again remove the foot of Israel from the land which I have appointed for your fathers—only if they are careful to do all that I have commanded them, according to the whole law and the statutes and the ordinances by the hand of Moses."

9 So Manasseh seduced Judah and the inhabitants of Jerusalem to do more evil than the nations whom the LORD had destroyed before the children of Israel. 10 And the LORD spoke to Manasseh and his people, but they would not listen.

11 Therefore the LORD brought upon them the captains of the army of the king of Assyria, who took Manasseh with hooks, bound him with bronze fetters, and carried him off to Babylon. 12 Now when he was in affliction, he implored the LORD his God,

and humbled himself greatly before the God of his fathers, 13 and prayed to Him; and He received his entreaty, heard his supplication, and brought him back to Jerusalem into his kingdom. Then Manasseh knew that the LORD was God. 14 After this he built a wall outside the City of David on the west side of Gihon, in the valley, as far as the entrance of the Fish Gate; and it enclosed Ophel, and he raised it to a very great height. Then he put military captains in all the fortified cities of Judah. 15 He took away the foreign gods and the idol from the house of the LORD, and all the altars that he had built in the mount of the house of the LORD and in Jerusalem; and he cast them out of the city. 16 He also repaired the altar of the LORD, sacrificed peace offerings and thank offerings on it, and commanded Judah to serve the LORD God of Israel. 17 Nevertheless the people still sacrificed on the high places, but only to the LORD their God. 18 Now the rest of the acts of Manasseh, his prayer to his God, and the words of the seers who spoke to him in the name of the LORD God of Israel, indeed they are written in the book of the kings of Israel. 19 Also his prayer and how God received his entreaty, and all his sin and trespass, and the sites where he built high places and set up wooden images and carved images, before he was humbled, indeed they are written among the sayings of Hozai. 20 So Manasseh rested with his fathers, and they buried him in his own house. Then his son Amon reigned in his place.

# The downs and ups of prison

Two very different inmates—or are they really so different?

### 'Joe' and 'Sam'

I have not met the first prisoner, 'Joe', though I know a lot about him. Much is written about his case and he has a high public profile on an international basis and is easily recognised. But I do know the second inmate, 'Sam', very well indeed. In fact he has become a close friend. His case, and especially his bizarre trial, made legal history and is in my legal textbooks. I knew his name from Stone's Justice's Manual, and from the main criminal law practice books, Archbold and Blackstone, long before I saw him listening to me when I first presented the gospel at his prison. I have had a lot of contact and fellowship with him since then.

### Murder plot thwarted—but—

Joe comes from a wealthy and influential family and had very caring parents. In fact, they—especially his father—spoilt him by making him the obvious favourite, causing the rest of his red-blooded siblings to envy and hate him. They saw him, with some justification at the time, as an arrogant 'wet'. Joe never tried to change his image of special privilege and measured aloofness—indeed he played upon it, seeing and promoting himself as the centre of his universe. He was more of a 'white collar' worker in his chosen comfort zone—if 'worker' was the right word for him. His older, hard-working 'blue collar' brothers found their abhorrence of him irresistibly strong and festering like an angry erupting sore. Finally they conspired to murder him. They kidnapped and bound him. The worst of their evil plans was thwarted at the eleventh hour, so they went to 'Plan B'. They callously sold him into the international human slave traffic that still plies its evil trade today. They returned home to lie to their grief-stricken father that they had found Joe's bloodstained clothes—rather like the defence argument in the infamous so-called 'coyote murder' case.

### The influences he needed?

A spoilt child like Joe could easily not have survived the cruel and rough world into which he had been involuntarily thrust. Hardship and Joe were never well acquainted! Happily for him, however, his ultimate buyer, an influential foreign dignitary, was neither perverted nor cruel and was not unjust. In fact he was quite reasonable and fair. After Joe had recovered from the trauma, shock and confusion of his terrible and involuntary changed circumstances, he was encouraged to work hard and was treated very well. Amazingly, Joe responded positively—perhaps freedom from the enemies in his family and isolation from pampering parents were the influences he needed. Or maybe it was the first time he had ever experienced job satisfaction, because it was probably the first time he had worked at a proper job.

Also Joe never lost his deep conviction that God would deal well with him in the end. He believed that God had made that clear to him, and so his underlying faith in the Lord was never broken. Obviously it was tested, as we shall now see.

## Sex—the devastating enemy

The vital outcome of all this was that Joe seemed to get closer to God than ever before. Suffering can do that for us. Joe never doubted God's existence, but had not demonstrated or enjoyed an excitingly contagious spiritual life. Maybe he had had it too soft for too long. It was too easy to hang on to the tails of the religion of his father and mother. His easy ride would change very soon. A young man with normal masculine drives, he began to develop mentally as well as physically. Temptation in the Middle East, where he was enslaved, was never far away. As his job performance improved and he grew in influence, so did his personal profile and reputation. His boss was a good and progressive manager and he gave Joe special assignments to match his expanding ability. These included legitimate ordinary daily contact with his boss's wife. Outwardly respectable, she was really a very immoral woman. Of sensual mind and desires, her overtures were not long in coming to Joe. Would Joe's growing faith crumble or triumph? Was he weak enough to look for God's strength to resist? Sex is God's wonderful gift in marriage, but can become a young man's devastating enemy. That is especially a danger when he is out of sight of parents and other restraining influences for good. That is why being away from home at university, or staying with certain friends, or taking a holiday without his parents, can lead a young man into strong temptation. Like chloroform, the nearer he lets sexual temptation get to him, the less he feels like resisting it. Many people—single and married—have fallen when confronted and attacked by this deadly dragon. Today, especially with disappearing moral standards, easy legislation, a dissolute media, and on-tap pornography, we need to heed the words of 1 Corinthians 10:12—*Therefore let him who thinks he stands take heed lest he fall*. Joe was certainly acutely aware of his weakness. Happily he was also growing in his awareness of his God.

## Becoming a man of God

So, by God's grace, Joe came through this temptation morally unscarred, though at great and instant cost to himself and his career. He flatly and immediately, and then continually and firmly, repudiated the older woman's advances and attempts to seduce him. He finally walked—in fact ran—out of the house. His boss's wife framed him. No doubt her abject failure to conquer a mere youth employee of her high-flying husband was combined with her anger and damaged self-esteem to vent her spleen on Joe. In an emotional charade, she convinced her husband that Joe had tried to rape her. Without PACE (Police and Criminal Evidence Act) in that country, justice was 'rough and ready' for a foreign nobody like Joe. Having worked up from slavery to being his boss's business director in comfortable surroundings, innocent Joe was suddenly incarcerated in a bare prison. In his unjust and unjustified suffering, God became more real to him still. The once spoilt Joe was beginning to turn into a man of God in the unchosen furnace of affliction.

## In prison

In prison, Joe learnt to get on with people and deal with the problems he encountered, rather than lamenting that he had to face them. He became so trusted in that eastern prison that its Principal Officer came to treat him more as a staff member than as a convict, though he was still not at liberty, of course. Joe was in effect a prototype of today's prison 'Listener'—an inmate who was trusted enough by the authorities to be asked to sit with prisoners and listen to their concerns. The Principal Officer delegated much responsibility to Joe, who never let him down. God was at work, however, in the circumstances surrounding his custody as well as in Joe's heart. Imagine Joe's feelings when two of the king's senior personnel were remanded in the same prison where he was now so influential. Despite feeling deeply his own frustrating injustice, he took a personal interest in the new inmates and their problems. They soon recognised that, as a God-fearing man, Joe was very different from the other 'cons'. Eventually they each confided in him about their terrible personal problems. He listened to them, prayed to God, and humbly but straightforwardly gave them answers which could only have come from God. As Joe had predicted, both the men were released by the king. Exactly as Joe had said would happen, one official was restored as the king's 'right hand man' but, sadly, the other was executed.

## He remembered Joe

Later, the official who had been restored to his office was struggling to find a solution to a big problem the king had shared with him. The king was demanding an answer. The official remembered how Joe had helped him and predicted accurately what would happen. He told the king about Joe. The king summoned Joe, who was sensitive enough to smarten himself up before appearing before him, and he shared his seemingly insoluble problem with the young man. Joe assured him that God would give him the wisdom to find the answer to the king's difficult dilemma—and proceeded to prove that was true! In counselling the king, and revealing the solution, Joe openly gave all the credit and honour to his greater King and Lord. God was glorified.

## From spoilt brat to life saver

The result? The king saw the immense potential in this fast-maturing and gifted, godly young man. He appointed him as his chief executive over all others. As Joe exercised that role with godly wisdom and transparent righteousness, the influence of the king and the economic and political strength of the whole country increased dramatically, even internationally. God, of course, was *the* reason why: but His chosen channel was a former arrogant and spoilt 'brat', who escaped from an evil murder plot to become an immigrant 'nobody slave', who began to be real with God and refused sin's allurements, who suffered unjust imprisonment as a result, who began to take God and the needs of others even more seriously than his own needs, and whose effectiveness for God in the prison and then in the palace changed world history! Not only was his own family and country of origin saved, along with his 'adopted' country, but many nations and people came to owe their lives and livelihoods to his wise and fair dealings in critical shortage situations. God was obviously and openly with him. The same God and Saviour is willing to help us to honour Him in our difficulties and circumstances.

Please don't tell me that when men and women in prison take God seriously it does not have great effects! You will by now, no doubt, have recognised 'Joe' as the son of Jacob and Rachel. (Genesis chapters 37 and 39–48.)

## 'Sam'—convicted of murder

There are not many obvious similarities between Joe and 'Sam'. Sam often attends the meetings run by DAYLIGHT in his prison. He is a 'lifer'—having been convicted of murder. (The safety of that conviction has been questioned by some and work on an appeal is currently in hand.) Another chapter deals with that situation a little, but suffice it to say now that he has become a mature Christian man in prison who is always looking out for others and keen to help. Sam is a 'Listener' in prison, and 'listens' sympathetically and well to other inmates' problems and grievances. That can be both challenging and depressing—especially when he has his own problems to face and is reminded of them. In that he is similar to Joe. Also like Joe, he is trusted by many of the staff who know him, as well as by all kinds of inmates. He seems to know everyone by name—officers and men—and genuinely cares for their welfare. I was with him in prison when we learnt that his appeal had unexpectedly failed. I saw how the spontaneous reaction of some experienced prison officers—for whom gullibility is a career-killer—reflected their respect for Sam's consistent and clear Christian testimony. That very evening, after phoning some people outside prison who had encouraged him and prayed for him, he bravely came to 'face the boys' at our Bible study and prayer time. Though surprised, rocked, subdued and disappointed, he participated in the discussion and prayer. Many inmates needing help or guidance turn to Sam. He is, unwittingly and unrecognised, one of the UK's best prison chaplains (though never able to be given that name, rank or salary!). He holds on to his daily reading of the Bible and prayer and seeks to honour the Saviour he came to know early during his sentence. We often go to his prison early to spend time with him before the Bible study begins. We invariably come away more blessed by him than he is by us. And he never misses making and sending cards for birthdays and Christmas, or asking how sick people are getting on when we have asked him to pray for them.

## 'It will be worth it all'

Sam will never be a monarch's 'right-hand man', like Joseph. In fact, the prospects of his getting out before the time laid down for the completion of his sentence seem doubtful, despite his exemplary conduct. Perhaps his consistent insistence on his innocence might count against him as it is not compatible with 'addressing guilt'. But however long he spends in human custody, he will be in glory one day with One who is far more important—the Sovereign Lord Jesus Christ, whose blood was shed to save him, whose grace is there to help him, whose Word is there to guide and feed him, whose Spirit is there to empower him, and whose people are there to pray for and support him. I personally think he should have received better justice this side of eternity, but in a million years from now he will know the truth of the old Christian song: 'It will be worth it all when we see Jesus.' The trials and temptations of his prison experience, which do not seem likely to be resolved on earth as happily as Joseph's were, will then seem very small and very far away. (As with Joe, God is testing him: will he be faithful to Christ despite the injustice of his situation?)

## An antique specimen or a looking glass?

It could be so easy to look at the story of Joseph as just that—a 'story'. And the temptation is there to slot his case, and Sam's, into our mind and memory rather like another documentary watched or another prison drama enjoyed on the television. We can take on the role of an enthralled spectator rather than an involved person who will pray and care. But we must ask ourselves some questions arising from these two cases.

First, are we entertaining any of the sins in Joseph's case that caused so much trouble? Are we unduly selfish and do we behave in a spoilt childish manner? Do we look down on others who are less privileged? Do we stick to our comfort zone rather than deal with the needs of others? Does envy and jealousy cloud our judgement and affect our actions?

Second, are we as uncompromisingly resistant to the overtures of appealing sin as Joseph was? Do we weaken if the temptation continues, or do we take drastic action to avoid it, even at personal cost?

Third, do we do the best we can in the circumstances in which we find ourselves, even when we hate them, and trust God for the outcome to glorify Him? In so doing, do we seek to do good to others en route, or do we bemoan our losses?

Fourth, can we be trusted to be faithful and hardworking when in positions of responsibility or in authority? If and when our influence or status grows, do we get humbly closer to God or more distant from Him in increased self-reliance?

Perhaps one reason why Sam is such a good witness in his prison is that his honest answers to those questions, by God's grace, would be much better than mine, and maybe yours. (He would not agree with that statement!) Even prison can be used by God to grow a man of God. We should pray that it will, again and again.

# Chapter 2

Genesis 39:

1 Now Joseph had been taken down to Egypt. And Potiphar, an officer of Pharaoh, captain of the guard, an Egyptian, bought him from the Ishmaelites who had taken him down there. 2 The LORD was with Joseph, and he was a successful man; and he was in the house of his master the Egyptian. 3 And his master saw that the LORD was with him and that the LORD made all he did to prosper in his hand. 4 So Joseph found favor in his sight, and served him. Then he made him overseer of his house, and all that he had he put under his authority. 5 So it was, from the time that he had made him overseer of his house and all that he had, that the LORD blessed the Egyptian's house for Joseph's sake; and the blessing of the LORD was on all that he had in the house and in the field. 6 Thus he left all that he had in Joseph's hand, and he did not know what he had except for the bread which he ate. Now Joseph was handsome in form and appearance.

7 And it came to pass after these things that his master's wife cast longing eyes on Joseph, and she said, "Lie with me." 8 But he refused and said to his master's wife, "Look, my master does not know what is with me in the house, and he has committed all that he has to my hand. 9 There is no one greater in this house than I, nor has he kept back anything from me but you, because you are his wife. How then can I do this great wickedness, and sin against God?"

10 So it was, as she spoke to Joseph day by day, that he did not heed her, to lie with her or to be with her. 11 But it happened about this time, when Joseph went into the house to do his work, and none of the men of the house was inside, 12 that she caught him by his garment, saying, "Lie with me." But he left his garment in her hand, and fled and ran outside.

13 And so it was, when she saw that he had left his garment in her hand and fled outside, 14 that she called to the men of her house and spoke to them, saying, "See, he has brought in to us a Hebrew to mock us. He came in to me to lie with me, and I cried out with a loud voice. 15 And it happened, when he heard that I lifted my voice and cried out, that he left his garment with me, and fled and went outside."

[16] So she kept his garment with her until his master came home. [17] Then she spoke to him with words like these, saying, "The Hebrew servant whom you brought to us came in to me to mock me; [18] so it happened, as I lifted my voice and cried out, that he left his garment with me and fled outside."

[19] So it was, when his master heard the words which his wife spoke to him, saying, "Your servant did to me after this manner," that his anger was aroused. [20] Then Joseph's master took him and put him into the prison, a place where the king's prisoners were confined. And he was there in the prison. [21] But the LORD was with Joseph and showed him mercy, and He gave him favour in the sight of the keeper of the prison. [22] And the keeper of the prison committed to Joseph's hand all the prisoners who were in the prison; whatever they did there, it was his doing. [23] The keeper of the prison did not look into anything that was under Joseph's authority, because the LORD was with him; and whatever he did, the LORD made it prosper.

# Can God use a 'lifer' or a Christian criminal?

## What happens if a prisoner seems to have finally 'blown it'?

### Death in custody

I do not know how it happens, but death in custody can be 'felt' throughout a prison. It is sad enough whenever a sick prisoner dies and the sad personal considerations of relatives coupled with procedural complications in prison can make it a nightmare. Sudden deaths caused by unexpected health problems are even worse. Relatively rare but savage cases of one inmate killing another seem to evoke a communal tsunami of guilt and fear. Then suicide—especially unexpected—depresses and troubles everyone. It crystallises the ultimate expression of despair and hopelessness, and the failure to make a telling difference. It seems that many different people feel part of the guilt and blame—often quite illogically. Tragically, a surprisingly high proportion of prisoners have been tempted to consider ending their own lives. One former long-term 'Listener' (a trusted inmate who listens to the cares, frustrations and problems of fellow detainees) confided that when he was in prison, once even *he* surveyed the prison carefully to see where he could locate the best place to hang himself. Prison can be a very depressing place, whatever the rights and wrongs of individual cases.

### 'Lifers' are often like you and me

But not every 'lifer' is depressed. Many in prison for murder, or serving other long sentences, come to terms with their future and settle in better than some shorter-term prisoners. Some are upheld by an amazing sense of humour, which helps them through. Most 'lifers' are not the archetypal criminals depicted in some TV dramas. Often, they are 'ordinary' people who reacted wrongly (and sinfully) in unusual circumstances at a particular time. Or perhaps they were in the wrong place at the wrong time with the wrong people. Although culpable and deserving punishment, they are no different from many other 'ordinary' people who would have reacted similarly in the same kind of circumstances. Of course, there is a sadly significant number of people who live to regret their graduation through relatively minor crimes to more serious ones. Sometimes it has become too late to realise that, like riding a bike, the best and safest time to stop is before you gather speed. Yet other people never seem to recover from a terrible childhood where abuse and lack of parental love have done much as a catalyst of evil in developing a criminal mindset and behaviour. That does not make such thinking and actions right. But it does help you to understand some inmates better. It also causes you to realise that, if your background was more privileged than many criminals, you ought to be very grateful and not take it for granted.

Many an 'ordinary Joe' might also have fought back in the pub car park brawl and gone 'over the top' in the heat of the moment. Often, only a black eye, a split lip, a broken nose or a few bruises might result—like in a rugby match. But sometimes someone dies. If the required criminal intent can be deduced, a stupid (and wrong) punch-up can turn into a murder that takes the life of one and wastes the life of at least one other person.

Talking of rugby, here is a case that does not deal with life sentencing, but which demonstrates how close you can be to getting a prison sentence when you might think you should walk away free. A normally robust club rugby forward punched an opposing player in the face. He said he did that to stop him repeatedly striking his team mate on the floor, a fact which was well witnessed. The punch, although a strong one that did serious damage, was only one punch. There were no feet and no head butts. The player was given a nine month prison sentence. Had he not hit the man so hard or so accurately in his desire to defend his colleague, his understandable plea of self-defence to protect another might have been effective as having demonstrated 'reasonable force in the circumstances'. Who knows? The same day, I am told by a rugby boffin friend of mine, in a high profile well-watched international match, one player repeatedly raked the head of another with his boot studs, causing wounds necessitating many stitches. That man had no legal action taken against him. Those roles could easily have been reversed. What is more, if the punched man had died and it had been held that grievous bodily harm had been intended, the offending player could have been given a life sentence for murder, not just nine months imprisonment. The point is that the player concerned was just an ordinary kind of man who played rugby.

## Bert's extra dimension of regret

Bert murdered his wife in his own bedroom after finding her in a compromising situation with another man. The man escaped, but his wife did not. Bert is still racked with guilt, not just because he killed the woman he loved, but because he despatched her into eternity when she was not ready to meet God. In prison Bert has trusted the Lord Jesus Christ and His finished work on Calvary's cross. I often recall some of his first words to me: 'If I had not come to prison I would never have come to Christ. But I cannot get out of my mind that I sent my wife to hell.' Becoming a Christian has changed his life but also brought him an extra dimension of regret. He is now a kind, gracious, well-mannered, much respected inmate in his prison. He knows the punishment for his murder as well as all his other sins has been taken by Jesus. But he also knows that the evil consequences of his wrong, though the act itself is forgiven, continue to ripple on.

## Sony—caring parents, but emotional and outrageous

Sony died in custody. (Only some of his details are related below—but we can all learn from them.) Sony was unusual. His caring parents taught him a lot about God and the Bible. The combination of his frequent mood swings and his genuine awareness of God, sometimes gave the impression that he was 'out and out' for God. At times he seemed zealous in his work for God, though even that often displayed a certain immaturity. He often bravely championed the cause of God's people against all the odds. He was certainly courageous—seemingly fearless, sometimes reckless. However, his intermittent extremism would have been better replaced by a daily, humble and quiet walk with his Lord. He needed to consider carefully and thoughtfully and pray over some of those truths about God which he had heard so often but never seemed able to take on board in a permanent way. Perhaps he liked too much to be centre-stage. He was often highly emotional and at times outrageous. But it must be said that he did get some remarkable results.

Very low on self-discipline, Sony showed that he was deceptively strong. He was rather like a seemingly 'normal' London prisoner I met whose 'friendly' handshake quite unexpectedly felt like a combination of an excruciatingly painful clamped vice and a cat's teeth! Revenge and personal vendetta motivated Sony's actions against those who opposed him. In fact, vengeance seemed to be a greater factor in his life than mercy or grace. This hardly seemed compatible with a life controlled by the Holy Spirit. His indiscipline was especially rampant in his relationships with women. For a man claiming a holy life committed to the Lord, his sexual exploits and liaisons were inappropriate and totally obnoxious to God. Also he rarely, if ever, seemed to show any sense of guilt or regret about his moral laxity—or about anything else he did wrong.

### Wasted and finished?

Finally this extroverted individualist with a very high public profile received a life sentence. Predictably, he was set up. He fell into a trap and was gullibly 'grassed' by a woman. His weakness and desire to live for the moment had come full circle. Probably even his own people considered him less harmful in prison than 'on the out'. Sadly, in prison he became blind and neglected. He seemed wasted and finished. Like so many people on the inside of prison, he seemed a pale reflection or a passing shadow of the strong resolute man he had appeared on the outside. Anyhow, it did seem that he was finally 'through'—washed up.

How very sad indeed! A blind, forgotten, failed, hopeless and seemingly helpless 'lifer'—with no remission or parole in mind. How very different now from those early hopes of his God-fearing parents! Everything seemed lost. Yet it was *now* that God stepped in to Sony's situation to use him to His glory. More of that soon.

### 'Peggy'

My wife, Phillippa, often visited an inmate, called 'Peggy' (the name and the circumstances below are deliberately blurred). Peggy, although a real Christian, committed a certain serious crime in her youth and her victim suffered. Peggy repented sincerely before God, and claimed the cleansing of the precious shed blood of Christ. Her deepening spiritual life and concern for the lost was evidence of her restored relationship and, after training, she moved abroad as a missionary. She was faithful and fruitful and all seemed blessed and well. Obviously she had regrets about the past and at times wondered if she had been sufficiently open with her victim about how sorry she really felt.

## Heart-stopping

Then the heart-stopping official letter arrived. She must return home to face questioning about her now long-past criminal offence. Unknown to Peggy, after all this time—and seemingly from a 'clear blue sky'—her victim had gone public. Peggy had neglected, in her earlier repentance, to really deal in depth with her victim, whom she knew well. Also in an endeavour to put things behind her, she had failed to ask her victim for forgiveness. Whatever the outcome, she should have done that. Who knows if her victim might have openly forgiven her and then have taken no further action in approaching the police? Now that was all surmise and speculation; it was too late.

Peggy never returned to the mission field from the police questioning. A small prison cell and unchosen inmate neighbours replaced her earlier joy and freedom of Christian service. She nearly cracked under the strain. Racked again by guilt and her negligent failure to have approached her victim—and maybe the police too—she thought God was through with her. Her family, friends and supporting church suffered terribly, too. So did the mission she had represented, apparently so well and faithfully. Public ministry was now impossible. Those deputation visits and missionary commissioning meetings mocked her like a fleeting dream.

## Humble and teachable spirit

Some months of inner torment produced, by God's grace, a very humble and teachable spirit in her. In her brokenness, she asked God to do the best He could with the remnants of her shattered life. She looked for others in prison to humbly witness to and help. A prisoner with enormous problems occupied the next cell. Peggy shared the gospel and showed God's love in helping in small ways. As a result, her new neighbour came to believe that God was real and cared for her. That prisoner—now released—is walking with Christ today as an infectious Christian witness, in the fellowship of a local Bible-believing church. Behind her tears and groans Peggy has played a big part in that.

And what of Peggy now? She is out of prison, with a very low profile and a daily walk of depth and humility with her Lord of mercy and grace. She continues to pray for and to help others. A good proportion of her very limited available income supports others who can work where she still feels disqualified to do so.

### 'When I am weak, then am I strong'

She is rather like Sony—whose full biblical name is Samson—in that at her lowest point, and despite her sinfulness, God used her for His glory and purposes. Samson, in his blindness and with his re-grown hair reminding him of his earlier holy Nazirite vow and his own personal godly heritage, achieved his greatest victory for Israel against the Philistines when, in captivity, he pushed the temple pillars down. (See Judges 16:18–31.) Peggy's achievements through God's grace are less spectacular—but eternally permanent. At least one soul (and probably many more) has been touched for eternity by Peggy's merciful, forgiving and loving God of faithfulness. For both Samson and Peggy, the truth that 'when I am weak, then am I strong' (2 Corinthians 12:10) has been demonstrated to be a personal reality. God wants our repentance, lack of confidence in self, and wholehearted trust in Him. He can do amazing things through failed sinners who trust Him and His faithfulness and move forward!

### Use the mirror and learn the lessons

Do you regard the account above as a spectacle or as a mirror? It should be the second. What lessons can we see there? First, it is vitally important to walk with God day by day. We 'grow in grace' (2 Peter 3:18) *not* 'jump through experiences'. Second, in the words of 1 Corinthians 10:12—which applies to women as well as men—'let him who thinks he stands take heed lest he fall.' Third, we reap what we sow (Galatians 6:7). Fourth, real repentance not only pleases God and blesses me, but it may also involve me in confession to others that may cost me dearly. Fifth, never consider that as a Christian you are out of God's merciful reach to forgive you or His encompassing grace to use you. He longs to do both. Sixth, our God is sovereign—He *really* is in control! Seventh, please pray for the salvation and blessing of lost and backslidden prisoners and that God will use his weak servants who take the gospel to them.

**NOW READ WHAT THE BIBLE SAYS IN JUDGES 16: 18–31:**

Judges 16:

18 When Delilah saw that he had told her all his heart, she sent and called for the lords of the Philistines, saying, "Come up once more, for he has told me all his heart." So the lords of the Philistines came up to her and brought the money in their hand. 19 Then she lulled him to sleep on her knees, and called for a man and had him shave off the seven locks of his head. Then she began to torment him, and his strength left him. 20 And she said, "The Philistines are upon you, Samson!" So he awoke from his sleep, and said, "I will go out as before, at other times, and shake myself free!" But he did not know that the Lord had departed from him. 21 Then the Philistines took him and put out his eyes, and brought him down to Gaza. They bound him with bronze fetters, and he became a grinder in the prison.

22 However, the hair of his head began to grow again after it had been shaven. 23 Now the lords of the Philistines gathered together to offer a great sacrifice to Dagon their god, and to rejoice. And they said: "Our god has delivered into our hands Samson our enemy!" 24 When the people saw him, they praised their god; for they said: "Our god has delivered into our hands our enemy, The destroyer of our land, And the one who multiplied our dead." 25 So it happened, when their hearts were merry, that they said, "Call for Samson, that he may perform for us." So they called for Samson from the prison, and he performed for them. And they stationed him between the pillars. 26 Then Samson said to the lad who held him by the hand, "Let me feel the pillars which support the temple, so that I can lean on them." 27 Now the temple was full of men and women. All the lords of the Philistines were there—about three thousand men and women on the roof watching while Samson performed. 28 Then Samson called to the Lord, saying, "O Lord GOD, remember me, I pray! Strengthen me, I pray, just this once, O God, that I may with one blow take vengeance on the Philistines for my two eyes!" 29 And Samson took hold of the two middle pillars which supported the temple, and he braced himself against them, one on his right and the other on his left. 30 Then

Samson said, "Let me die with the Philistines!" And he pushed with all his might, and the temple fell on the lords and all the people who were in it. So the dead that he killed at his death were more than he had killed in his life. 31 And his brothers and all his father's household came down and took him, and brought him up and buried him between Zorah and Eshtaol in the tomb of his father Manoah. He had judged Israel twenty years.

# Paterson's penalty

## A really 'evil' prisoner with an amazing story

### 'Evil' Paterson

You will meet a unique character in this chapter. This man and his well-documented legal case are legendary across the world. Even men in prison with no legal background—other than personal experience!—know quite a lot about 'Evil' Paterson, even if they forget his real name. That such an evil man could be slotted into the staggering timing of the main event of this story, with its repercussions throughout history, makes your blood run cold. That such terrible injustice and legal abuse of process perpetrated by others could have unwittingly embraced and benefited him is a deep stain on the face of human civilisation. At the same time it provides a wonderful picture of forgiveness. You must read on to see how this all works out. This chapter will be based on history and developed with a little imagination, just to flesh out the bones! When personal imagination is superimposed significantly on the historical facts of this case, clear notification will be given! In any case it should be obvious.

No one has been able to research successfully what Paterson's real first name was. I almost said 'Christian name', but there was absolutely nothing Christian about Paterson. His adopted and preferred name, 'Evil', described him perfectly and was used widely. He was held in fear by all 'types and conditions of men', large and small, rich and poor, intelligent and ignorant, and high and low. Yet at the same time that his very presence struck terror into many people, he was a man with a huge charismatic appeal. I find that hard to explain, but it was so. Perhaps some people were too frightened *not* to follow him. That fear made them do so with apparent gusto and loyalty. Maybe mobsters following a Mafia 'godfather' would understand that. Just as the East End Kray twins had (grudging?) admirers and very loyal supporters, so did the far less sophisticated Evil Paterson. Had he been a little more sophisticated, he could have been described as a cross between a Sicilian 'godfather' and the Kray twins. But he was not sophisticated.

Paterson, as well as being a criminal involved in many unsavoury situations, was a murderer. How many people he had violently despatched to an untimely eternity is still not known. It probably will never be known. But he was much more than a murderer. He led violent and criminal uprisings, too. In the wake of those tidal waves of lawlessness, all sorts of crime, cruelty, abuse and injustice followed. His ragged and rugged band of villains was probably responsible for more killings, crimes and suffering than he was. But he led and incited them. He was both the architect and the midfield football player rolled into one. He could not be said to be the 'brains' behind the outfit—that would not have described him accurately— but he was a sinister motivator of others to follow what he did.

## Death row

In fact, on the day in question that we will examine more closely, two men thought by some to be his closest conspirators and criminal cronies started their last day on earth by waiting on death row with Paterson. (You have to guess where they were!) Their gripping story merits totally separate treatment, but suffice it to say now that the three of them were counting down the hours before life would finally ebb out of those bodies which had become such instruments of wickedness and harm to so many people. They had at last received their just judgement from a court of law. But the worst was still to come—God's eternal judgement was yet to fall. And God as judge never misses a fact, never misunderstands a line of thought or reasoning, never can be misled by a witness, and never is persuaded by a wrong argument, however clever it may seem to be. And He is the only judge who needs no jury—He knows exactly what happened, why, when, where, how and by whom.

Dr Samuel Johnson said that the death penalty 'concentrates the mind wonderfully'. He might have been less philosophical and more panic-stricken if *his* heart, like Paterson's, had been violently thumping away its relatively few remaining beats while awaiting death to be imposed upon him by others. But he had a point: when faced with death, a thinking man cannot but also think about eternity. How can he pretend it is not at least a possibility even if he is not yet fully convinced of its reality? Surely the fear of the unknown is nearly as great as the fear of the known? That uncertain fear is only eclipsed by the dark and cold shadow of the eternal reality that 'after death, the judgement'. On a far lower level, just doing time in prison has acted as a catalyst for a number of prisoners. It has speeded up their more urgent thinking through the issues of right and wrong, innocence and guilt, life and death, heaven and hell, and pardon and punishment. That is why, under God's grace, some turn to Christ in prison who might never otherwise have considered God seriously when on the other side of the bars. I have heard a number of prisoners explain in different words how they have found salvation in Christ inside prison. God met them as they began to think seriously through their shameful past. It was then that they began to understand their unworthiness and the words of Isaiah 1:18 became so pertinent to them—'*Come now, and let us reason together*', *says the* LORD, '*though your sins are like scarlet, they shall be as white as snow; though they are red like crimson, they shall be as wool.*'

If the serious concentration of thought and reflection upon one's need for forgiveness and reality focuses sharply in prison because an incarcerated convict feels his (or her) weakness when just facing imprisonment, then imagine the hugely more intense and terrifying pressure on a condemned criminal as he watches seconds tick away on death row. Every passing grain of the sands of time seems to represent a part of his passing life.

## Imagine how he felt

How can anyone accurately describe Paterson's true inner feelings, fears and thoughts? What happened to him is clearly and accurately documented in this leading case in legal history. I doubt if the annals of legal reporting have ever recorded a greater breach of justice.

But let us seek to get inside this wretched man's mind. He cannot be very different from many hard 'macho' men I have met 'inside'. So I will merge them into 'Evil' Paterson, just to set the scene for what really happened. I am using my imagination, now, but the reality could have been a lot worse than I am portraying here.

With his throbbing head held in his horny hands and a lump in his throat so colossal that he found it hard to accept that it was part of his own body, and with deep regrets, he travelled nostalgically and tearfully down 'If Only' lane. Why and where did he go so wrong? It was true that his home life had not been brilliant—his father was a rough, uncaring bully but his mother loved him even though she found it very hard to cope. But his two brothers had not ended up 'inside', as he had, even though they were by no means saints. In fact they never even got near the fringes of criminality that seemed to attract 'Evil' so easily. Many other people had far worse lives than he had. So why had he gone so wrong?

Now he desperately wished that he had never hung around with the crowd that led him increasingly into wrongdoing. He remembered the first time he cowardly thrashed a terrified and weaker solitary youth, while 'Evil' was surrounded by his jeering mates. He had always hated being bullied himself, and vowed never to do it. But now he found that he, too, was bullying others. Petty theft gave way to violent robbery in a relentless sinking spiral of lawlessness and crime that *en route* took away the few remnants of morality he then possessed. He was a good talker, too. He had a silver tongue. That linked with his strong physique and overpowering personality to make him a spontaneous leader of others who would not think for themselves or who, if they did, were frightened to say so. They either respected or admired, or liked or feared him—probably all four at different times in different combinations.

He remembered one day hearing someone speaking on the hillside. He was on his own then. It was a big public meeting of just very ordinary people of all ages. This speaker seemed to radiate sincerity, earnestness and peace. He was urging men and women to 'repent and believe'. Paterson had never thought about that much before. He didn't really even know what those words 'repent and believe' meant, if he was honest. (But he was rarely honest anyhow—not even to himself.) As he listened, hiding at the back of the crowd, his realisation of his selfish and wayward life seemed to upset and worry him for a while. He heard that to be forgiven he must own up to his own wrongdoing (that amazingly persuasive and appealing speaker called it 'sin') and come openly to God, yielding to Him and asking Him to forgive him and take control of his life to change it. That is the only part of the message he heard at the back of that crowd, before he slunk away: but it stayed with him. He never discussed it with others—that would not have been 'macho'. But he often reflected on it in his quieter moments on his own.

'If only, if only, if only,' he whispered to himself in that miserable cell. Then it happened!

## Out!

The awaited footsteps were heard in the clanky corridor, coming nearer. They seemed to accelerate in speed and in volume and then stop outside his thick and very secure cell door. Then he heard the muffled voices of the prison officers—getting louder. Then came the last bang on the cell door that he would ever hear. Finally, there was the grating sound of keys turning in the huge lock. Soon it would be all over for him. 'If only!'

'Paterson!' Knowing his violent reputation and great strength, four officers had come to confront and collect him. 'Paterson, get up!'

This was it. Now he really wished he had turned from his sin and turned to God. Now he lamented that he had gone deeper and deeper into sin. He wished …

Then the bombshell unexpectedly exploded in his thoughts and shattered the numbness of his confused and panic-stricken thinking— 'Paterson, you're *free*! You're *walking*!'

Free? Walking? Not to die? The eruption of that impossible good news ran like hot lava through his now fragile mind which just so recently had been morosely and dejectedly reflecting on his past and on his sad and wicked mistakes. Free? Free? It could not be. No—they were mocking him. How could he go free?

'Don't you take the mickey out of me, mate.' Though shaking like a leaf inside, his rough words matched his gnarled and stubbly face and his solid muscular frame. 'Don't you dare take the mick out of me!' He thrust out his chin and tried to sound as threatening as ever. But he felt weak inside.

Without further words, the officers led him away to the custody desk. Paterson was bewildered and hardly noticed that he was handcuffed to two of the men. He collected his few belongings, which had been taken from him after he had come into custody. He never thought he would see them again—or need them. He signed for them with a trembling hand, which was very unusual for him. He never remembered the walk from the custody desk to the outside door. But then he was *out*! Out in the sunshine. Out by himself. And no one had even told him why. He could not believe it. He did not know whether to laugh or cry so he did neither.

## Dying

Let my imagination continue. I said, 'Out in the sunshine.' But before long, the sun would be completely blacked out. (That part really is historical fact, and not imagination.) Before that staggering event, (still my imagination!) Paterson found himself strangely drawn to the public execution where he was supposed to die with his two other criminal friends—his convicted inmates. Like him, they were due to die right now. He saw them dying, hanging crucified on Roman crosses. They were cursing and swearing and insulting the man on the middle cross. Yes! It was *him*. There between them was that man—the same man whom he had heard talking about repentance and sin. He still seemed to radiate peace, even as He died. But why was He there? He was not one of 'Evil's' gang. A sign over His cross said 'The King of the Jews'. (The most amazing fact of history is that Jesus did die on the cross, between two convicted criminals, for our sins.)

Did Paterson (which, like Barabbas means 'the son of the father') really see and hear the Lord Jesus Christ teach? Did he witness His crucifixion after his release from prison? Did he hear Jesus say, 'Father forgive them' or 'It is finished' or any other of His seven sayings from the cross? I do not know. The Bible is silent on this point.

Would he have heard his two intended co-victims at first blasphemously cursing and insulting the Lord Jesus Christ? If so, he must have noted the sudden and deep change in one of them as he resisted the peer pressure of his taunting and unrepentant friend. Maybe he heard him turn to Jesus and say 'Lord, remember me when You come in Your kingdom.' Would he have caught Christ's reply to him, 'Today, you will be with Me in paradise'?

I asked an inmate at a large London prison service how he thought he would have felt if he had been Barabbas, and if he had been released and had seen Jesus dying on that central cross that should have been his. What did he think his emotions would have been? What would have gone through his mind?

How did he reply? Very quietly he almost whispered, 'I'd think I should have been there instead of Him.' Another volunteered seriously, 'Jesus was in my place.'

I told the inmates that everyone who had truly turned from sin and come to Christ for forgiveness felt and knew like that. The death of Christ on that cross becomes even more personal to the sinner trusting Him for forgiveness than it could even have seemed to Barabbas on that day. (Read Matthew 27: 15–26, 38–54.)

## How others put it

The Bible says:

'Christ bore our sins in His own body on the tree [the cross]' (1 Peter 2:24) and 'We esteemed Him stricken, smitten by God, and afflicted. But He was wounded for our transgressions. He was bruised for our iniquities; the chastisement for our peace was upon Him—the LORD has laid on Him the iniquity of us all.' (Isaiah 53: 4–6).

One hymn says:

Because the sinless Saviour died
My sinful soul is counted free.
For God the just is satisfied
To look on Him and pardon me.

And a children's chorus puts it so well:

Wounded for me. Wounded for me.
There on the cross He was wounded for me.
Gone my transgressions and now I am free.
All because Jesus was wounded for me.

Do you know that Jesus Christ died for sinners like you? Have you turned to Him as your Saviour?

**NOW READ WHAT THE BIBLE SAYS IN MATTHEW 27:15–26, 38–54:**

Matthew 27:
15 Now at the feast the governor was accustomed to releasing to the multitude one prisoner whom they wished. 16 And at that time they had a notorious prisoner called Barabbas. 17 Therefore, when they had gathered together, Pilate said to them, "Whom do you want me to release to you? Barabbas, or Jesus who is called Christ?" 18 For he knew that they had handed Him over because of envy. 19 While he was sitting on the judgment seat, his wife sent to him, saying, "Have nothing to do with that just Man, for I have suffered many things today in a dream because of Him." 20 But the chief priests and elders persuaded the multitudes that they should ask for Barabbas and destroy Jesus. 21 The governor answered and said to them, "Which of the two do you want me to release to you?" They said, "Barabbas!" 22 Pilate said to them, "What then shall I do with Jesus who is called Christ?" They all said to him, "Let Him be crucified!" 23 Then the governor said, "Why, what evil has He done?" But they cried out all the more, saying, "Let Him be crucified!" 24 When Pilate saw that he could not prevail at all, but rather that a tumult was rising, he took water and washed his hands before the multitude, saying, "I am innocent of the blood of this just Person. You see to it." 25 And all the people answered and said, "His blood be on us and on our children."

26 ¶ Then he released Barabbas to them; and when he had scourged Jesus, he delivered Him to be crucified …

38 Then two robbers were crucified with Him, one on the right and another on the left. 39 And those who passed by blasphemed Him, wagging their heads 40 and saying, "You who destroy the temple and build it in three days, save Yourself! If You are the Son of God, come down from the cross." 41 Likewise the chief priests also, mocking with the scribes and elders, said, 42 "He saved others; Himself He cannot save. If He is the King of Israel, let Him now come down from the cross, and we will believe Him. 43 "He trusted in God; let Him deliver Him now if He will have Him; for He said, 'I am the Son of God.'" 44 Even the robbers who were crucified with Him reviled Him with the same thing. 45 Now from the sixth hour until the ninth hour there was darkness over all the land. 46 And about the ninth hour Jesus cried out with a loud voice, saying, "Eli, Eli, lama sabachthani?" that is, "My God, My God, why have You forsaken Me?" 47 Some of those who stood there, when they heard that, said, "This Man is calling for Elijah!"

⁴⁸ Immediately one of them ran and took a sponge, filled it with sour wine and put it on a reed, and offered it to Him to drink. ⁴⁹ The rest said, "Let Him alone; let us see if Elijah will come to save Him."

⁵⁰ And Jesus cried out again with a loud voice, and yielded up His spirit. ⁵¹ Then, behold, the veil of the temple was torn in two from top to bottom; and the earth quaked, and the rocks were split, ⁵² and the graves were opened; and many bodies of the saints who had fallen asleep were raised; ⁵³ and coming out of the graves after His resurrection, they went into the holy city and appeared to many. ⁵⁴ So when the centurion and those with him, who were guarding Jesus, saw the earthquake and the things that had happened, they feared greatly, saying, "Truly this was the Son of God!"

# When prison peer pressure collapsed

## How one man finally resisted peer pressure and is now very glad that he did

### 'Sinny'

If ever there was an inmate whose name and nickname told the story of his life, Steve Lawless was that man. With a name like 'Lawless' you might have joked that he was bound to end up in criminal ways. If you came across him, however, you would not dare to joke about his name or risk anyone telling him that you had joked about him. He was not only openly evil in his language and actions: his motives were recognised to be so sinister that he was happy to be known as 'Sinister Steve', which over the years shortened from 'Sinister' to 'Sinny'. Anything with 'sin' in it was a most appropriate name for him. He was a volcanically violent and compulsively dishonest schemer as well as a rabble-rouser and bully who imposed his evil will uncompromisingly on his many weaker peers. Surprisingly, he was also easily led as long as the person leading him was bad enough and strong enough for him to follow. His long 'CRO' (criminal record) started in 'YOIs' (Young Offender's Institution) and was monotonously full of violent public order offences, robbery with violence, 'GBHs' and 'ABHs' (convictions for grievous bodily harm and actual bodily harm), common assaults and assaults on the police, as well as sickeningly repeated convictions for burglary and theft. Up to his current state of being found guilty—which carried the death penalty at that time and had been upheld after a lengthy appeal process—he had amazingly managed to escape convictions both for murder and for attempted murder, though prison gossip was rife about how he had kept these off his record. His mentor in evil, a man he alone called 'Pat', had 'higher qualifications' in these respects than he had. ('Evil' Paterson's story is covered in the previous chapter.)

Chapter 5

## Dud Dexter

Sinny's constant companion and follower was Dud Dexter. Of Middle Eastern origin, he was physically bigger and stronger than Sinny, and possessed a muscularity and athleticism that reflected regular and serious workouts in the prison gym and that often seemed to mark him out in this prison from many (though not all) of his flabbier and weaker fellow inmates. But Dexter (as Sinny always called him) was weak on the inside and was quickly and increasingly controlled by his dominating mentor. If a point had to be made in the wing of the prison where the two men had their cells—just two cells apart—Dexter would be Sinny's messenger and, if necessary (which was not often the case, as a threat usually did the trick), his executioner. Dexter was believed to be the strongest man and one of the two best fighters in the prison. Very few would want to challenge that reputation and so he also had a following made up of violent and strong men. His conviction for a brutal dual murder, also recently unsuccessfully appealed after a long time of waiting, had done much to enhance that reputation. That had suited Sinny very well, in running his 'scams' involving trading drugs and pornography for possessions, larger portions of meals, other surrendered privileges, and the virtual enslaving of those who dare not do other than Sinny or Dexter decreed.

## What Sinny never knew

Sinny never knew that Dexter had unsettling moments of great misgivings and guilt. That guilt was not only because he sometimes thought about the victims of his own robbery and violence—both personal and in near-riot situations—but also because he had come to like some of the inmates whom he had to bully in order to keep in with Sinny. At times, in his shared cell with Jim Greenhalgh (just an 'ordinary' compulsive thief and drug addict), he had found it hard to get to sleep and had decided to tell Sinny that he was through with adding yet more wrongdoing to his own violent record of failure, wickedness and selfishness. But somehow, when he met up with Sinny, he lacked the 'bottle' and so continued under Sinny's vile influence. That recognition of his own cowardice made him feel even guiltier. In fact he often seemed even harder than Sinny had required, just to be seen to be independent. But he was not a happy man on the inside. He knew he was even less free in his heart, than in the more obvious area of his enforced custody in that huge prison. As his date for public execution drew nearer, he wished he had never been involved in crime. He thought back, with a nostalgic hopelessness, to his earlier years when his caring and loving mother had taught him the Ten Commandments and urged him to live a righteous life. Those days had long since gone. He found it hard to understand how Sinny could remain so hard and seemingly unaffected either by his wrongdoing or by the imminent death penalty that awaited him also.

## Hardness in prison

Perhaps I could digress a little at this stage to comment on hardness in our prisons today. Obviously, many men and some women appear to be as hard as they can as a defence mechanism. This approach is by no means limited to prison but can be found in school playgrounds or in corporate boardrooms. Those using this mechanism think like this: 'If the others reckon that I really am tough and that I will react strongly and decisively to opposition, I may not get bullied or bossed around.' Others use their hardness as a badge to impress others, both fellow inmates and officers. Some of the really hard men do not have to make a point of it, however, and seem remarkably laid back.

We know of one prisoner in a northern prison who rules the roost there. Yet in talking to him after a meeting you would think he was a run of the mill teacher or a bank employee. He always courteously asks if we would like a cup of tea or coffee after the meeting, though it is often someone else who brings it after he merely raises an eyebrow at his chosen waiter. And he is not even physically strong or well built. It all seems very strange—even to the experienced chaplain.

Others whom we have come across have such obvious physical power, coupled with the 'gift of the gab' and even (sometimes) a cultured approach. They do not need to put on an act to make a point. In fact, one such man took pity on a bullied weakling and protected him. That man had a peaceful passage through that part of his sentence. Why that protective instinct for that man? Who knows? Life is not always logical or predictable in prison.

Often the hardness on the outside is a veneer to cover vulnerability within. One convicted murderer admitted to us that he is too scared not to appear hard and aggressive. He hates himself for putting on an act, and struggles with that as he comes to a growing understanding of what it means to become a Christian. He talks of tears quite openly when with us, but never hints at it in front of his fellow inmates, even in a Christian meeting we run at his prison.

But tears are not really the issue. Remember Esau, who 'found no place for repentance, though he sought it diligently with tears' (Hebrews 12:17)? Many a convicted man has wept tears of remorse, without bending the stubborn neck, flexing the selfish knee, or surrendering the sinful heart in repentance. Repentance is marked by a surrender of the will, and earnest prayer that God will turn the repentant sinner from his or her sin, so that the Saviour whose blood was shed for forgiveness of sins takes up residence as Lord of the life, motives and actions. Tears can include tears of repentance, but they certainly do not constitute it. We need to pray for a brokenness for sin and a crowning of the Lord Jesus Christ as personal Saviour and Lord, regardless of whether people are in prison or outside prison.

### Even harder to admit to being a sinner?

Perhaps the hardest thing that some prisoners can encounter is to be seen to be weak in admitting that they really were wrong and need forgiveness. (Again this is not limited to men and women in custody. In fact, we sometimes struggle with it too, don't we?) Everyone who turns from sin and casts themselves wholly on Christ crucified for forgiveness and salvation battles with pride *en route*. The way up is down, and to admit not only sin, but also the blame and guilt that deserve eternal judgement does not come easily—especially in today's 'self-esteemed society'. Many of us have peer pressure to deal with—at school, or university, or in the office, or on the work floor, or in our neighbourhood, or among our close friends. But in prison, where the 'macho man' seems to command a huge respect and following, it seems harder for an inmate openly and consistently to admit his wrongdoing with real regret, sincere remorse and, even harder, true repentance that makes a difference. He begins to swim against the tide and will be misunderstood and his 'bottle' questioned by some. He will often be made an outcast because he is under new management and now follows the One who is the Truth and commands a life of selfless love to be lived before others. That is hard anywhere—but especially in prison where the criminal environment is obvious. It is paradoxical—in one way, prison makes it easier to admit sin superficially, because the 'mask has slipped' for all who have been found out and apprehended. But it is also easier to justify it and even glory in what one has 'achieved' in crime, compared to other criminal 'under-achievers'.

## Dave

Take Dave as an example. His inmate friends could not understand it—or him. Since his conversion, he was certainly not 'in' with them and they could no longer regard him as one of their 'mates'! As one of the most muscular and physically strong men in the prison—a quality which was combined with a very alert mind, a facility with words and an apparent softness that could be deceptive—Dave certainly had been 'in' with the 'in crowd'. Now he showed no interest at all in the scams, the porno, or the drugs that were formerly part of his prison life. From the start of his new Christian life, he had the advantage over many prisoners that very few (if any) of the prison bullies would dare to stand up to challenge him physically to protest against his new lifestyle. Coupled with all that, it was well known that he now helped and supported the men around him. One prisoner had intended to follow a precarious but lucrative career, after release, as a contract killer. He later told me that he was going to pack it all in because Dave had spoken to him and helped him. This man had sensed a new peace in his new friend. Dave, in fact, was a fitness freak. He counteracted his withdrawal from doubtful, and not so doubtful, things which still occupied many inmates, by training them in the gym to get them in shape! That way he maintained a positive 'neutral' contact with them.

Dave could hardly believe his conversion himself. 'What's happened to me?' he even asked. Little wonder that Dave's co-convicts, like those who the apostle Peter said 'pursued a course of sensuality, lusts, drunkenness, carousing, drinking parties and abominable idolatries', were 'surprised that [he] did not run with them into the same excesses of dissipation' any more (NASB—1 Peter 4:3–4). Even though Dave went through a very testing time through very serious and unexpected heart illness—a time when he felt very low—it seemed as if he was seeking to walk with the Lord.

The sad thing is that since leaving prison, and after a promising start in which Dave was welcomed, accepted and helped by Christian friends and a caring church with which he was put into contact, Dave 'disappeared'. A few days before that he had seemed to be going on well. We discussed, in a café near his lodgings, how he could tackle some problems he was facing, with God's help, and applied common sense. He seemed relaxed and happily determined. We even sought to discuss Bible passages by phone. However, a family dispute, a failure of the authorities to get his paperwork through in time for him to claim his rightful benefits when he needed them, and continued serious ill health did not help him.

We at DAYLIGHT feared that he might not be going on with Christ. He had our phone numbers and address and we had made visits to see him and even passed on some needed financial help from loving Christians. We hoped that our fears would be groundless and we continued to pray for him and for renewed contact. Then we heard that he was back inside a large London prison. We wrote, trying to arrange to visit him, but there was no reply, despite the intervention of a chaplain we know well. Then Phillippa 'stumbled across' a phone number when filing some papers. She remembered that the number belonged to one of Dave's friends. She phoned it and found that Dave was out of prison, and in a probation hostel, not far from us. She contacted the hostel and two days later we were with Dave. He told us his story.

He had been 'breached' by his probation officer. (That means his licence for early release had been revoked through alleged bad conduct.) He had spent six months 'inside' as a result. Eventually he had an appeal heard before the parole board and a judge. The judge stated there was no evidence whatsoever to support Dave's having been breached. He was given an immediate unconditional discharge, but was still under probation until the expiration of his sentence date.

Although not guilty of any new crime, Dave had not been going on with the Lord as he should have been. Why had he not been in touch with us? A letter from him, which 'coincidentally' arrived the morning of the day that we had arranged to meet him (and mailed well before Phillippa's phone call) explained:

'I am truly sorry that it has taken me so long to write back to you but I have felt embarrassed by my return to prison and I felt that I needed to clear my name first. I felt quite lost, I hope you understand that it's not that I didn't want to contact you but that I felt I had let you both down.'

We renewed the contact often and then one day found he had been unexpectedly breached again, despite committing no crime and keeping the rules well. Why was he breached? Because the medication described by the prescription sent to his hostel said he should be taking ten items of medication, whereas a more recent prescription had reduced it to two. Those medications had caused a dangerous amount of excess weight to be added to his formerly athletic frame. Dave was asked by the hostel to sign a disclaimer regarding those two items, on their promise that it would not prejudice him. He did that and then found that the hostel had instigated a breach for not being willing to take prescribed medication! Back to prison! At the appeal hearing, Dave was instantly released because the judge found that his licence conditions had expired and he should not have been breached for allegedly breaking them! Again Dave went back to the same hostel, where he was treated most unhelpfully and unsympathetically both by the hostel and his probation officer. (I stress here that many hostels and probation officers seek to do a good job and help as much as they can in the circumstances.)

Although Dave had been told he was not under licence at his recent appeal, and although he committed no crime, he has recently been breached yet again because he felt he was being so harassed (especially as a prisoner 'not under licence') that he weakened and finally stayed out of the hostel. Atthe time of writing, he is again back in prison, never having committed a further crime, while his very compassionate lawyer seeks to get a hearing expedited to argue his case yet again. Dave still seeks to go on with the Lord, although it seems to a number of observers that he has been set up to fail by others.

It can be so hard for even truly converted men and women on release, and they need so much prayer and support. We know the heartache of seeing men and women—apparently truly converted—no longer showing the Christian life-style they seemed to show in prison. (That is why I do not rush to claim 'converts' or ask them to testify until their changed lives show their conversion clearly.) But God's grace is still operational and the Lord is not through with Dave yet. He is not perfect, of course, but we rejoice that at least he committed no further crime and that, under extreme provocation from those who should have helped him, he never reacted against them in the way that most people would have done in his situation. With all his failures, we can see God's hand on Dave, and look forward to his release in the coming months when no licence conditions will apply.

## Back to Sinny and Dexter—and peer pressure

With, I hope, a better understanding of hardness and peer pressure in prison (and perhaps the even harder path outside the bars for those who leave prison), we return to Sinny and Dexter. Few folks had as vile a vocabulary as Sinny and Dexter, and they used it to the full in prison. Even on the day of their execution, when they met a man who was lamb-like in his demeanour, but who showed himself to be lion-like in his strength and courage, they insulted this prisoner with their obnoxious language. He was so different from their fellow inmates and especially from themselves.

But how did the saga of Sinny and Dexter conclude? Dexter's opportunity to take his stand against his sin and against his evil mentor came. He took it by God's grace alone. Sinny and Dexter were indeed being put to death at the prescribed place of public execution. They were surprised to find that the lamb-like man they had insulted was the last minute substitute for 'Evil' Paterson, their gang leader. Paterson should have died with them, but the lamb-like man was nailed to the cross that should have been Paterson's. Dexter was on the man's right hand—for 'dexter' originally meant 'on the right hand'. Sinny was on his left—the original meaning of 'sinister'.

At the start, they both continued their vile insults. In fact they found they were part of a chorus of wolf-like howling against this inoffensive man. The crowd, apart from a small sad-looking group of women and one man with them, took up the cruel taunts of the religious leaders, who orchestrated the evil symphony. Even the criminals' guards joined in—except the 'Principal Officer', the Roman centurion.

## Dexter suddenly changed

Then Dexter suddenly changed. He seemed to understand what was really happening. As God's grace touched him he seemed to be given a remarkable insight (as did that quiet Roman centurion in charge of the condemned prisoners) that the Man on the central cross, the Lord Jesus Christ, was the Son of God and a totally righteous man. He was paying for sins that He had never committed. That included the sins of Dexter, one of the dying criminals on one of those three crosses. He admitted to himself and to God the awfulness of his sin and realised that he was being punished justly for his own sins against God and against others.

He turned to Jesus alone for personal forgiveness. At last, and only with his receiving God's grace in his heart for the first time in his life, he was given strength openly to resist the peer pressure of his lost and sinful mentor. He confronted him, shouting from the right-hand cross to the left-hand one and being heard by the Lord Jesus, that both the criminals were getting the punishment they deserved. He gasped to his hardened friend that Jesus was different—there was no wrong or guilt in Him to be punished. He was dying for people like them. He told Sinny to stop the insults and the blasphemy, and humbly prayed a startling prayer from his heart to his Saviour.

'Lord, remember me when You come in Your kingdom.' From the depth of His suffering, Jesus immediately assured the wretched but now repentant man that he would be with Him that very day 'in Paradise'.

Christ's mercy, love and grace divided one crucified man from the other, overcoming peer pressure and pride. One, refusing repentance and faith, died a lost and condemned man. The other, who turned, was forgiven and accepted. He would be with Christ for ever. Eternity would show how vital was that repentance and grace to the one, and how tragically sad was the hardness of sin to the other.

## The historic account

Obviously, I have indulged my imagination to put this moving historical event into a modern prison context. But the basic principle and action is historical. Luke 23:39–43 gives us the essential factual account from God's word:

Then one of the criminals who were hanged blasphemed Him, saying, 'If You are the

Christ, save Yourself and us.' But the other, answering, rebuked him, saying, 'Do you not even fear God, seeing you are under the same condemnation? And we indeed justly, for we receive the due reward of our deeds; but this Man has done nothing wrong.' Then he said to Jesus, 'Lord, remember me when You come into Your kingdom.' And Jesus said to him, 'Assuredly, I say to you, today you will be with Me in Paradise.'

(Read more around this historical happening in Luke 23:32–47 and Matthew 27:38–54.)

## The ultimate victory over sin and pride

Paul tells the Ephesians that 'by grace you have been saved through faith, and that not of yourselves; it is the gift of God, not of works, lest anyone should boast' (Ephesians 2:8–9). If works could save us, pride would swell to such an infinite level of evil that heaven would not and could not be heaven. The theme in eternal glory will be that Jesus, as a spotless slain Lamb, has shed His blood to save us. The focus of heaven will never fall on the good works of its forgiven occupants!

The dying thief, 'Dexter' in this chapter, recognised that he had nothing to give him false confidence of acceptance or adequate grounds of justifying merit before a holy God. No good works, no giving to others, no church attendance, no religious ceremony such as baptism, and no Bible reading or prayer meeting attendances could ever make him right with God. He was saved solely by the blessed and pardoning combination of mercy and grace received personally and directly from his Saviour, who was bearing his sin and its judgement on that central cross. That must be the ultimate victory over pride and sin: not only *could* he do *nothing* to save himself, but he never even had the *opportunity* to do anything!

Mercy and grace gloriously triumphed in Christ's last meaningful conversation on earth before His death. And please note that it was with a condemned criminal! How can anyone say that Jesus is not compassionately interested in criminals coming to Him?

**NOW READ WHAT THE BIBLE SAYS IN LUKE 23:32–47, MATTHEW 27:38–54:**

Luke 23:

32 There were also two others, criminals, led with Him to be put to death. 33 And when they had come to the place called Calvary, there they crucified Him, and the criminals, one on the right hand and the other on the left. 34 Then Jesus said, "Father, forgive them, for they do not know what they do." And they divided His garments and cast lots. 35 And the people stood looking on. But even the rulers with them sneered, saying, "He saved others; let Him save Himself if He is the Christ, the chosen of God." 36 The soldiers also mocked Him, coming and offering Him sour wine, 37 and saying, "If You are the King of the Jews, save Yourself." 38 And an inscription also was written over Him in letters of Greek, Latin, and Hebrew: THIS IS THE KING OF THE JEWS. 39 Then one of the criminals who were hanged blasphemed Him, saying, "If You are the Christ, save Yourself and us." 40 But the other, answering, rebuked him, saying, "Do you not even fear God, seeing you are under the same condemnation? 41 "And we indeed justly, for we receive the due reward of our deeds; but this Man has done nothing wrong." 42 Then he said to Jesus, "Lord, remember me when You come into Your kingdom." 43 And Jesus said to him, "Assuredly, I say to you, today you will be with Me in Paradise."

44 Now it was about the sixth hour, and there was darkness over all the earth until the ninth hour. 45 Then the sun was darkened, and the veil of the temple was torn in two. 46 And when Jesus had cried out with a loud voice, He said, "Father, 'into Your hands I commit My spirit.'" Having said this, He breathed His last. 47 So when the centurion saw what had happened, he glorified God, saying, "Certainly this was a righteous Man!"

Matthew 27:38:

Then two robbers were crucified with Him, one on the right and another on the left. 39 And those who passed by blasphemed Him, wagging their heads 40 and saying, "You who destroy the temple and build it in three days, save Yourself! If You are the Son of God, come down from the cross." 41 Likewise the chief priests also, mocking with the scribes and elders, said, 42 "He saved others; Himself He cannot save. If He is the King of Israel, let Him now come down from the cross, and we will believe Him. 43 "He trusted in God; let Him deliver Him now if He will have Him; for He said, 'I am the Son of God.'" 44 Even the robbers who were crucified with Him reviled Him with the same thing. 45 Now from the sixth hour until the ninth hour there was darkness over all the land. 46 And about the ninth hour Jesus cried out with a loud voice, saying, "Eli, Eli, lama sabachthani?" that is, "My God, My God, why have You forsaken Me?" 47 Some of those who stood there, when they heard that, said, "This Man is calling for Elijah!" 48 Immediately one of them ran and took a sponge, filled it with sour wine and put it on a reed, and offered it to Him to drink. 49 The rest said, "Let Him alone; let us see if Elijah will come to save Him."

50 And Jesus cried out again with a loud voice, and yielded up His spirit. 51 Then, behold, the veil of the temple was torn in two from top to bottom; and the earth quaked, and the rocks were split, 52 and the graves were opened; and many bodies of the saints who had fallen asleep were raised; 53 and coming out of the graves after His resurrection, they went into the holy city and appeared to many. 54 So when the centurion and those with him, who were guarding Jesus, saw the earthquake and the things that had happened, they feared greatly, saying, "Truly this was the Son of God!"

# Don't forget the 'screws'

## God and the prison officers

### 'Key' people!

Prison Officers are genuinely 'key' people in prisons. Affectionately or not, as the case may be, they are referred to as 'screws' by the inmates. They are not the only ones issued with keys but they are the main ones and every officer has them. Their job is not the most popular, and whatever they do will be wrong for someone. They will be regarded as being either too hard or too soft, too strict or too lax, too stand-offish or overfriendly, too much a stickler for details or too negligent of detail, too miserable or too frivolous, too disrespectful to visitors or over-familiar with them, too insubordinate to seniors or lacking in initiative, too scared or too aggressive, and so the list could go on and on. There will always be someone looking at officers in a different way. Many inmates appreciate the hard job the POs have to do and that most officers and SOs (their Senior Officers) or POs (the Principal Officers) try their best to be fair and reasonably approachable. But there will always be some offenders in custody who try to string them along. Similarly, there will doubtless be a small proportion of officers (as in any job) who are not pleasant and make no attempt to deal with the inmates as people. For every officer who does not seem to do a good job, there must be very many more who do theirs well, cheerfully and helpfully.

This chapter is intended to introduce you briefly to a number of prison officers. As with the rest of this chapter and book, identities have been blurred deliberately and any names given of individuals or prisons are not accurate.

### The 'awkward man' on the desk

He seemed to me to be awkward. I had clearance to draw and use the keys at his prison but there was a failure to mark my ID card accordingly to indicate I had that concession. Bill (the officer concerned) knew I had drawn keys before on a number of occasions. I had been going there for years. But his rulebook said effectively 'no marked ID card = no keys'. In some other prisons, his colleagues might well have stretched the point—but not Bill. I saw him as difficult. The trouble was that as I began to react to him, in a way that did not honour the Saviour I had come to proclaim, he also saw me as being increasingly awkward. He was right. He knew that I knew that he was under authority, and that what he was doing was actually completely by the book. We had words—obviously nothing serious when compared with the language and demeanour of the world—but I knew I was wrong as I bubbled up inside and made a few sarcastic comments. My reactions were showing. Happily for me, someone else with keys escorted me to the chapel where I was due to conduct a discussional Bible study for 'lifers'. I had done that many times before as well and had often been blessed from the Scriptures in sharing Christ with the inmates. That night they asked why I did not have keys. I told them. In all fairness I did not criticise Bill at all, but just gave the facts. Some of them readily volunteered their clearly held opinions, which I will quickly pass over! We then got on with the Bible study together.

We came to the biblical principle of the need to confess your sins to God and put things right with others. I could not carry on that Bible study without telling my class of men, who were mainly convicted of murder, that I had acted terribly as a Christian and had just asked God to forgive me for it and cleanse me from it. Furthermore, I intended to ask the forgiveness of the person I had offended as soon as I saw him again. After I explained in answer to their questions, they could hardly believe that I was talking about *Bill!* 'Oh, *him*,' one said, 'he deserves what he gets.' I pointed out that he did *not* deserve it and that I was wrong. I had come to learn that the cleansing from sin through Christ's shed blood, following confession of sin, was such a mercy and a blessing. And anyhow, I owed him an apology. (At the next study they asked me if I had apologised! I am glad I had!)

I have rarely seen a man's face change more quickly than when I told Bill I was truly sorry and asked for his forgiveness. Others were at the gate then, too. The security hatch did not allow room to shake hands through the strengthened glass, so we tipped fingers with each other and smiled. I am glad to say I have come to like that 'awkward man' immensely and he has been very helpful to me since. Occasionally we have shared a short word through the glass on things that matter most. I pray for him. The whole episode was a timely and humbling reminder to me that I need a clean heart to go to serve the Lord. That can only ever be accomplished by God's marvellous mercy and grace in Christ. I cannot lead others out of their prisons if I am still sinfully slouching around my own.

### Gerard—can you give me some booklets, please?

The above question is, I am very happy to say, often asked in prison. My colleagues and I are always very happy to respond positively. It is good to give to men who sometimes are locked up for twenty-three hours, some clear statement of the gospel to consider during that time.

But this request was different! First, it was one of the officers who asked. Again, that is by no means rare. They often take booklets offered and not infrequently instigate the request. I have been asked by various officers for outlines of talks given and for books to be sent to them on the resurrection of Christ and on the Bible. It is always a joy to oblige. So that is all OK! But this officer was a woman. Still nothing unusual there—there are many women officers in both men's and women's prisons. Most do a very good job. Yes, but this request came to me during a service in which I had already spoken and while I was sat with the men in the main body of the church. Aaahh! That really *is* unusual. Why did she ask for the booklets then? It was because this dear lady officer had noticed the irrational behaviour of a troubled man at the back. He had called out loud a number of times (not maliciously) during my talk in the second service on what it means that Jesus is 'Saviour'. He actually listened quietly between his shouts and applauded me at the end! At the end of my talk, I offered them evangelistic booklets to take away. This lady officer decided she would bribe him out of the church by offering the booklets now and quietly leading him away. That would avoid further disturbance around him and her colleagues would not need to spoil the service by physically making him leave. That dear lady did what two strong men could not do—she got him to leave peacefully and he took some good Christian literature with him to read. I found out afterwards that she was a Christian too—a bright and caring witness in a dark place.

### 'That man kept me going on!'

One very immoral and very needy man came to trust Christ in prison and had a desire to read the Bible. He was helped by a number of people to come to faith and to go on with the Lord. One of them was an ordinary officer at his prison. The prisoner told me that when he had questions on the Bible and God he would often not wait to raise it in a letter. Instead, he would find this officer and ask him. Obviously they both had to be careful to observe certain protocols of conduct and relationships between staff and inmates. Neither of them abused that in the slightest. The inmate's comment later was, 'That man kept me going on! I took all my hard questions to him and he answered them all.' The converted inmate is now out and really going on with Christ and having a positive impact on his family. That officer's kindness and concern is part of God's success story, though it will never get on his annual assessment.

## 'You're wasting your time!' or 'Please give me some for the lads on the wings'

But now and then you might find an officer who seems a little hostile. This could happen in any walk of life. The one I have in mind was very big and very muscular. Frankly he looked as if he could have been in custody himself. (By the way, I once wrongly thought a Prison Chaplain was an inmate, so I am a very bad judge!) While I waited to shake hands with well over a hundred men, he 'invaded' my personal space. Literally—as well as metaphorically!—looking down on me (I am around six feet tall), he sneered that I was wasting my time. He insisted that the men only came to trade in drugs and not one of them was a Christian. On hearing the last statement, I assured him that, in that case, I was in exactly the right place and prayed that there would be some Christians by the end of the service. I challenged him about his relationship with God and his need of forgiveness. He, too, was just as lost as the inmates were and, like them and me, he needed a Saviour. Although he rudely rebuffed me I noticed he was reading the booklet 'How can God accept me?' as the service progressed. He has often been in my prayers since.

By contrast what a joy to go to a Young Offenders' prison where one SO comes after the service and takes as many booklets as he can hold. He then goes to give them to the lads on the wings who did not come to the service. He thinks that the booklets will do them good and that they need a positive input!

## The officer who watched a high profile prisoner —and got converted!

Do you remember reading about one PO in charge of a dangerous and explosive group of criminals—murderers, robbers, violent thugs and rabble rousers—and watched one of them so closely that he got converted? In fact that was also true of one of the 'cons' he was watching! This man had absolutely no Christian background and no obvious belief in God or the Bible. Like many people, he had probably never had a serious thought about God in his life. But he carefully observed the demeanour of one of those in his charge as he had to face some horrible circumstances. He could tell from the man's actions and words that he was very different from the others. Interestingly, that is exactly how the offender also got converted around the same time, despite the continual insulting and blasphemous peer pressure of others. Do you remember who those two were?

## He was 'anti-God' but now loves Him and tells others about Him

One PO was well known for his strong dislike of Christianity. His views were often aimed at the members of the chaplaincy at his prison. One of them—a godly Salvation Army man—prayed and prayed for the man and showed Christian love as well as sharing the gospel. The result? There is now a Bible study for officers in that prison with some coming to Christ and others seriously seeking the truth. Who was the first member of it? The 'anti-God' man who was the first to trust Christ and share his good news with other POs.

## The governor of a small prison was suicidal

A lot of prison governors began life as prison officers. One such governor—I'll call him Mr Philips—became suicidal at his prison when he wrongly thought all his prisoners had escaped or were escaping, following serious damage suffered to the prison. Happily for him, a bright witnessing Christian prisoner told him that all was in order and everyone was still there. Mr Philips asked that prisoner, who was very well known, and his co-accused (also a Christian) what he needed to do to know God's salvation. He was told to trust in Christ. Mr Philips did exactly that, and so did all those in his home. They all believed in Christ and were saved, and also were baptised. That man then bent over backwards to look after his Christian prisoners who actually had suffered a huge miscarriage of justice. Have you read about him too?

## The opportunity carries on

Well no doubt you deduced that the 'governor', Mr Philips, was the Philippian jailer (Acts 16:25–34), converted after an earthquake had first followed and then preceded the clear presentations of the gospel in prison by Paul and Silas. They were not only in prison but also kept in the stocks! The character I referred to earlier in this chapter was the Roman Centurion in charge of those soldiers guarding the criminals to be crucified. This wrongly included Jesus, on Barabbas's cross, and rightly included the two criminals, who were crucified on each side of Jesus. The comments of the Centurion about Jesus (by the way, the Centurion had no Jewish or Christian background) were, 'Truly this was the Son of God' and, 'Truly this was a righteous Man.' He knew from God that Jesus was fully God and also fully man. In common with the dying criminal who prayed 'Lord, remember me when You come in Your kingdom', he knew that Christ must be dying for the sins of others, not for His own, because he knew Jesus was 'righteous'. (Look up the passages in Luke 23:32–47 and Matthew 27:45–54.)

May the opportunities continue for Christians to share, sensitively but clearly, the Lord Jesus Christ with Prison Officers! I cannot believe that the apostle Paul, chained to his guards in Rome, did not chat to and recommend his Saviour to them! Sometimes officers ask personal questions directly, and I recall the privilege of talking with and praying with two of them in shock after they had just discovered the prison suicide of a young man. But for many, the hardness of the job and the genuine need to remain objective and deal at arm's length can form barriers to the possibility of being rightly vulnerable to such sentiments as 'I really am sorry—I was wrong', or, 'I am too weak to hack this on my own: I need God.' Prayer and the gospel can achieve that by God's gracious power and love.

## The prisoner they could not hold

Finally, there was one set of powerful and well-trained officers on guard duty who were to keep the Man under their charge inside. And that was although there were plenty of them, and although the high profile place in which He was being kept was very well secured and certified officially to be secure. Not only that, but the Man they were guarding was already correctly certified as dead! Read about it in Matthew 27:62 to 28:20 and then consider the following words:

*Death could not keep its prey!*

Jesus my saviour!
He tore the bars away!
Jesus my Lord!
Up from the grave He arose
With a mighty triumph o'er His foes.
He arose the Victor from the dark domain
And He lives for ever with His saints to reign.
He arose! He arose!
Hallelujah! Christ arose!

It is with the utmost confidence that those who have the privilege to present Christ crucified and risen from the dead do so. That is true whether the message is delivered to prisoners, to officers, or to anyone and everyone else—inside or outside prison. Our unique Saviour is alive and offers eternal life to those who turn from sin and trust in Him! Our confidence is in Him who still today gives prisoners of sin lasting and real freedom!

# Chapter 6

Matthew 27:

62 On the next day, which followed the Day of Preparation, the chief priests and Pharisees gathered together to Pilate, 63 saying, "Sir, we remember, while He was still alive, how that deceiver said, 'After three days I will rise.' 64 "Therefore command that the tomb be made secure until the third day, lest His disciples come by night and steal Him away, and say to the people, 'He has risen from the dead.' So the last deception will be worse than the first." 65 Pilate said to them, "You have a guard; go your way, make it as secure as you know how." 66 So they went and made the tomb secure, sealing the stone and setting the guard.

Matthew 28:

1 Now after the Sabbath, as the first day of the week began to dawn, Mary Magdalene and the other Mary came to see the tomb. 2 And behold, there was a great earthquake; for an angel of the Lord descended from heaven, and came and rolled back the stone from the door, and sat on it. 3 His countenance was like lightning, and his clothing as white as snow. 4 And the guards shook for fear of him, and became like dead men. 5 But the angel answered and said to the women, "Do not be afraid, for I know that you seek Jesus who was crucified. 6 "He is not here; for He is risen, as He said. Come, see the place where the Lord lay. 7 "And go quickly and tell His disciples that He is risen from the dead, and indeed He is going before you into Galilee; there you will see Him. Behold, I have told you." 8 So they went out quickly from the tomb with fear and great joy, and ran to bring His disciples word. 9 And as they went to tell His disciples, behold, Jesus met them, saying, "Rejoice!" So they came and held Him by the feet and worshiped Him. 10 Then Jesus said to them, "Do not be afraid. Go and tell My brethren to go to Galilee, and there they will see Me."

11 Now while they were going, behold, some of the guard came into the city and reported to the chief priests all the things that had happened. 12 When they had assembled with the elders and consulted together, they gave a large sum of money to the soldiers, 13 saying, "Tell them, 'His disciples came at night and stole Him away while we slept.' 14 "And if this comes to the governor's ears, we will appease him and

make you secure." [15] So they took the money and did as they were instructed; and this saying is commonly reported among the Jews until this day.

[16] Then the eleven disciples went away into Galilee, to the mountain which Jesus had appointed for them. [17] When they saw Him, they worshiped Him; but some doubted. [18] And Jesus came and spoke to them, saying, "All authority has been given to Me in heaven and on earth. [19] "Go therefore and make disciples of all the nations, baptizing them in the name of the Father and of the Son and of the Holy Spirit, [20] "teaching them to observe all things that I have commanded you; and lo, I am with you always, even to the end of the age." Amen.

# Roses from the rubbish tip

**The amazing things that can come out of prison**

### The rubbish tip

I remember feeling sad and highly offended one day in court when a prisoner with whom I was dealing was described by the chairman of the magistrates as 'a waste of space'. He had just lost an application for bail—and rightly so in the circumstances, as it did seem from his past record that he would probably re-offend if let out on bail. The prosecution's unchallenged version of the facts had been presented. That chairman's statement might well have been one of the hidden triggers in my mind that made me so glad to accept the invitation I received later to be involved in Christian prison work. No one is ever 'a waste of space'. Each man and woman is made in God's image, however marred by sin and wickedness, and can become a forgiven and changed person by faith in Christ.

So the reference in this chapter to prison as 'the rubbish tip' is simply to indicate that prison is a place where people end up when there is nowhere better for them to go. The alternatives have been tried and society has decreed that this is the only place now suitable for our offending fellow human beings.

Having said that, prisons really are not nice places at all—even the best of them. If you gather together in one place all the individuals whom society has incarcerated to remove them from the public—whether you see that as penal or as reforming—the fact is that putting all the 'bad eggs' together cannot make an omelette which is safe or nice to eat! There are younger and older offenders who get schooled in crime and 'scams' just by being in prison with others. Often two inmates share a cell designed years ago to house one person. That cell is basically a toilet for two in which they eat, sleep (if and when they can), and live. The rubbish tip image is not so far away here.

### How about the 'roses'?

Given the gathering together of so much criminality in a society where Christian morality has been ignored, rejected, despised and legislated against (take homosexuality, for example), it is amazing that any roses at all can grow on this custodial rubbish tip. Yet they do grow, and some examples of that now follow.

## Roses from bread

One of the great privileges of going to prison so often and meeting so many people—some of them again and again—is that I have made some good new friends. I would not necessarily lend my car or house keys to every such 'friend' on release! But to a select handful I would—and have. One inmate, who has been wonderfully brought to Christ in prison, obviously felt that he owed me something. That was because I had the privilege of sending him some good Christian books to read in prison and he could not reciprocate. He is out, now, and Phillippa and I have stayed with him and his family on a number of occasions. When he was 'inside' he got permission to present me with a beautiful pink and green rose decoration, which still adorns my window ledge. He made it in prison from the rather doughy bread saved from his prison dinner. I think the colour came from putting something dyed red into water and then dipping the rose in it. Here was a literal rose from prison's rubbish tip. The same man sent me pictures he had painted. Since release on licence he recently gave me, as a birthday present, a magnificent painting of a stag which he called 'Gerard of the glen'! In prison he made a Fabergé-style decorative egg that I understand would cost a lot to buy in a jeweller's shop. But the best 'bloom' that came from this man was neither that bread rose nor that Fabergé-style egg. It was seeing his new Christian life blossoming in prison. I cannot give the details as he could easily be traced. Suffice it to say that amid much disappointment and hardship—most of it not of his own making—he not only came to know Christ but also began to grow in his Christian faith. His reading and endeavour to understand the Bible and his praying and helping others became daily priorities. He had been truly suicidal, but became known in his prison for his even temperament, his cheerfulness and his selflessness. Each day he would get alongside and help his fellow inmates and share with them something of what Christ had done for him and meant to him. He began to help at and lead the prisoners' Bible studies. He would invest some of his (very small) financial compensation for his prison job by buying biscuits to give away at the Bible studies. If you like, he bribed (without corruption!) men to go to the Bible studies. We were able to link him and his wife with a very caring church that loves the Lord, the Bible, and people. God's grace has been seen in restoring his marriage and rebuilding the family. But even so he has ongoing struggles with smoking. Also, it seemed easier in prison, with fewer responsibilities, to achieve discipline in his quiet time than now, when he has to get up early for the work he so much appreciates. He wrestles with his quiet time—haven't we all done that at times? Converted prisoners need at least as much prayer out of prison as they do when they are in. But, nevertheless, here is another rose of God's grace which grew on the unpromising rubbish tip of prison! I am privileged to call him my friend and brother.

## More 'roses'

Two other prisoner friends are excellent painters. From time to time, they send my wife and me a painting. One of the men finds writing a difficult chore, so he saves up a few letters and then sends me his latest painting with a few lines on a sheet. A few lines of writing are harder for him to produce than to paint an eagle or a landscape. The other rose in his life is that after a cancer operation, more ill health, and being moved around the prison system, he is now at a Category D prison and anticipating and preparing for release. His brother was formerly supportive and promised to find him a job. As release approaches, he has distanced himself from our friend, who came to know the Lord in prison some years ago. With one or two hiccups, he walks with the Lord each day, despite finding smoking a problem, which he would like to give up but finds hard to do so. When you consider how far this dear man has come, it makes you less critical of some remaining weaknesses. It is always good to see him in the congregation when I go to preach at his prison.

The other man who paints was a big blessing to the one just mentioned when both were in custody at the same prison. He is remarkable. He is extremely clear on most points of Christian doctrine and biblical teaching despite having had little or no Bible knowledge when he was convicted. He has continued to grow spiritually even in some prison chaplaincies that have not shared his evangelical faith. Despite maintaining his innocence as strongly now, after years of walking with Christ and helping other inmates, as when he entered prison as a non-Christian, he is still serving a long sentence. He is three quarters through it now. His appeal was turned down, much to my surprise and the dismay of those who knew him best. There is a lot more to him than sending nice paintings he has done. When he was going through a time of real darkness after his appeal was refused, he continued to help other needy inmates. As a result of his involvement and care, he was almost solely responsible for stopping one inmate committing suicide. When discussing the disappointment of the refusal of his appeal, he volunteered that he had come to understand more clearly why God would have him stay in prison. 'If I had not been here,' he said, 'it seems that Ian might now be dead.' This same man who, when hearing the comment made to him, 'I think you have had rough justice—you have had it really hard,' answered, 'I would not have missed this for anything.' When questioned more closely—because it took him years and years of determination even to get an appeal heard—he explained that he had come to know Christ in prison and added, 'I would not have given Him five minutes' thought outside.' Remember that he is serving a long sentence for a vicious crime he denies having committed and for which no forensic evidence was offered. His conviction was solely on the grounds of circumstantial evidence. Perhaps one day his case can be reassessed and maybe the advance in DNA technology might help him. Be that as it may, through all this God has brought His eternal blessing into this man's life. Whether he will get out of prison without serving the full term, I do not know. I am absolutely sure that he will be in heaven in a billion years' time and, of course, long after that! Eternity is very long by definition! Here is another of God's roses that He has grown on the custodial rubbish tip.

## A semi-humorous side to prisoner relationships

It is not surprising that one prisoner can make a strong impact on another one in prison, whether for good or for bad. Sometimes there is a semi-humorous side to it. A man who is a bit of a rogue and a rebel at heart—a very strong man—is someone for whom I have a lot of affection, and have had numerous occasions with him when we have talked about Christ. I will call him 'Jake'. For internal prison reasons, Jake had to be moved from one prison to another and stay at a third prison *en route* overnight. Jake was tired and glad to get to bed when the men were 'banged up'. Sharing his cell was a rather cocky, much younger man. 'I am in here for shoplifting,' he proudly boasted. Then, equally cockily, he eyeballed Jake and said, 'What are you in here for?' Jake was by now undressing to occupy the bottom bunk for his much-craved night's sleep. Perhaps the young man noted the bulging muscles of the man who had once been a professional footballer. Quietly, and without even looking at the youngster sitting at the table, Jake muttered, 'One murder and two attempted. Now please excuse me I want to get to bed.' Jake noted the young man look scared and shocked, but he got into bed himself and had a good night's sleep. When he awoke in the morning, Jake told me that the young man was sitting where he was the night before still shaking with fear. He had been unable to go to sleep because of his criminal companion. Jake asked him if he had been awake all night, and laughed when he said he had. The rest of Jake's comments are not for publication!

## The amazing story of one committed man

Let me refer to another prisoner who shared his prison space with a co-inmate. Unlike Jake, he was not a murderer. In fact, there was much talk that he was one of the relatively few prisoners who really should not have been convicted at all. (He was another person whom I believe was wrongly in prison. I think that even my close friend who is a Christian lawyer would agree about that on the facts of his case.) His name was Evan. He was a vigorous but elderly man and was an exemplary inmate. A prisoner who is in denial about the offence for which he has been convicted can find that his privileges are withdrawn. Also, he might well not get parole until he is seen to address his re-offending. That can prove to be a big problem if he knows he did not offend! Should he tell the truth and risk losing his privileges and the prospect of release on parole? Or must he lie and go through the prison system's 'addressing guilt' hoops to please the authorities and have a better chance of parole? Evan could not honestly address his guilt in the prescribed way because he claimed he was innocent. But that did not stop him looking out to help others in that prison.

## Proffy

In custody with him there was a rough-working lad, nicknamed 'Proffy', who had been on the run, but had been apprehended. He was basically a thief. Whether that would eventually have graduated into other crimes, who could say? Evan befriended Proffy and spent a lot of time talking to him. What Proffy did not realise at first was that Evan was a keen Christian. Before long, however, Evan was sharing with his younger friend that Jesus Christ had died on the cross to forgive his sin and cleanse him from it. He also explained that Jesus was alive and through the power of that risen life could enter Proffy's life and keep him going straight. Better still, he would receive eternal life at the moment he turned to Christ. That would carry on throughout eternity. But Evan made it very clear and plain that Proffy could have no forgiveness, no eternal life and no heaven unless he was prepared openly to confess his sins to God and forsake them. He could not hold on to the Saviour and at the same time hold on to his sin. One of the many evidences of living faith in Jesus Christ would be that, where possible, he would ask forgiveness from those whose things he had stolen. Also he would undertake to restore what he had taken, wherever that was possible.

To cut a long story short, Proffy repented of his sins and received Christ in his life as his Lord and Saviour. Things began to change remarkably. Among other things, he now did everything he could to help and encourage his older father-like friend, Evan, with whom he prayed and studied the Bible each day. That was in addition to his own daily quiet time in God's Word and in prayer.

## Theft from his boss

As they grew closer in Christian fellowship, Proffy explained to Evan that he had stolen from a certain Mr Friend, who was his boss and also a Christian. That was why he was on the run. Proffy knew he was forgiven by God and now wanted to pay back to his boss what he had stolen. My guess is that he did not have the means to return all he had stolen. Evan was clear on the steps Proffy should take, based on his new life with Christ. An amazing 'coincidence' in God's sovereign plan was that Evan already knew Mr Friend! In fact it was Evan whom God had used to lead Proffy's boss to Christ. He had stayed with him before as his guest!

As the day of Proffy's release came closer, Evan and Proffy prayed together and discussed a lot about how Proffy should act. They agreed that he should go straight back to Mr Friend and confess to him the theft and ask his forgiveness. Also he was to offer to pay back what he had stolen, even if it took time to do it. Evan would write an accompanying letter to Mr Friend for Proffy to take with him.

## What Proffy probably did not know until later!

Proffy left Evan and went straight to Mr Friend. That was a journey in which he probably prayed every step of the way! His older friend could not stop praying either from the prison cell, which he did not deserve. I cannot say for sure what the reaction and course of action were from Proffy's boss, but I would be very surprised if he did not take him back joyfully and unconditionally, not only as an employee again, but also now as a brother in Christ. He would have recognised that now, as Christians, Proffy and he had the same eternal family relationship in Christ as they had with Evan. My guess is that he might well have accepted whatever money Proffy had to pay him, but that he probably let him off the rest. Why? Well, although I doubt if Proffy knew it as he delivered that sealed letter, it contained an offer from Evan to pay the debt. The letter made that very clear! Mr Friend owed a lot to Evan, including, under God, his own salvation. Oh—and one other thing! I cannot be dogmatic but I doubt if Proffy carried on as a slave any more. That is what he had been. I think he might well have been received as a son as well as a brother. Again, Evan's letter to Mr Friend might well have set the scene for that.

## Paul, Onesimus and Philemon

Do you recognise the story of this rose growing on that particular prison rubbish tip? Evan is the apostle Paul, for whom the gospel (or 'evangel') was always his prime concern. Proffy is short for 'profitable', the translation of the name of the runaway slave Onesimus. (He became very profitable spiritually as a result of knowing the Lord.) Why call Philemon, to whom Paul wrote the short letter sandwiched between Titus and Hebrews, 'Mr Friend'? Because the root of that Greek name means 'friend'. I am sure Philemon and Onesimus became as firm friends of each other as they both were with Paul. They were all brothers in Christ.

**NOW READ WHAT THE BIBLE SAYS IN PHILEMON 1:8–25:**

Philemon 1:

8 Therefore, though I might be very bold in Christ to command you what is fitting, 9 yet for love's sake I rather appeal to you—being such a one as Paul, the aged, and now also a prisoner of Jesus Christ—10 I appeal to you for my son Onesimus, whom I have begotten while in my chains, 11 who once was unprofitable to you, but now is profitable to you and to me.

12 I am sending him back. You therefore receive him, that is, my own heart, 13 whom I wished to keep with me, that on your behalf he might minister to me in my chains for the gospel. 14 But without your consent I wanted to do nothing, that your good deed might not be by compulsion, as it were, but voluntary.

15 For perhaps he departed for a while for this purpose, that you might receive him forever, 16 no longer as a slave but more than a slave—a beloved brother, especially to me but how much more to you, both in the flesh and in the Lord.

17 If then you count me as a partner, receive him as you would me. 18 But if he has wronged you or owes anything, put that on my account. 19 I, Paul, am writing with my own hand. I will repay—not to mention that you owe me even your own self besides. 20 Yes, brother, let me have joy from you in the Lord; refresh my heart in the Lord.

21 Having confidence in your obedience, I write to you, knowing that you will do even more than I say. 22 But, meanwhile, also prepare a guest room for me, for I trust that through your prayers I shall be granted to you.

23 Epaphras, my fellow prisoner in Christ Jesus, greets you, 24 as do Mark, Aristarchus, Demas, Luke, my fellow labourers.

25 The grace of our Lord Jesus Christ be with your spirit. Amen.

# Letters from prisoners

**Somewhat different from Paul's prison letters
—but well worth reading!**

### Another excellent example of 'roses from the rubbish tip'

In the chapter you have just read, we have considered just a few wonderful
'roses' that have grown from prison's 'rubbish tip'. There is a huge bed of
roses in the form of books and letters written in prison. That bed embraces
the most beautiful blooms of all—Paul's prison letters—but includes other
writings that have moved many readers. John Bunyan wrote what became
the world's second best seller, 'Pilgrim's Progress', from prison. That is a
book inspired by God's inspired and infallible book, the Bible. Many other
letters and books have come out of the deprivation and suffering caused by
curtailing a person's freedom. In one sense, Anne Frank's diaries were from
her personal prison, for example. Or think of Corrie ten Boom's
challenging account of being in a Nazi concentration camp. Or read
*Miracle on the River Kwai.*

Prisoners' letters can rarely reflect the same degree of unjust punishment
or persecution as innocent victims. However, civilised governments have to
admit that there is bound to be a small percentage of people who are wrongly
convicted and imprisoned. That is why we have an appeal system to seek to
remedy such injustices that come to light. I am convinced that the appeal
system also lets some who should be free men and women—albeit not
many—languish in custody. But that is the nature of even the best of human
justice, painful as it is for the relatively few who suffer unjust imprisonment,
and for their deprived and saddened loved ones. There is no such thing as
absolute justice this side of eternity. Juries and judges of all ranks can and do
make honest mistakes. God the Judge never makes a mistake. Each person
will appear before Him one day to be judged for all wrongdoing—unless he,
or she, has repented and taken refuge in the entirely righteous Saviour God
who bore the penalty of sin on the cross for those who will trust Him.

Having signalled that some prisoners are wrongly detained, it has to be
recognised then that most in custody in civilised countries which seek
(albeit imperfectly) to uphold the rule of a basically righteous law cannot

claim to be suffering there without a degree of blame. Some inmates will fully admit that they are getting what they deserved. 'You do the crime and you do the time!' is a well-accepted statement by lots of men and women detained at 'Her Majesty's Pleasure'. (I hate that phrase—and, writing as an Englishman, I doubt if our gracious Queen is at all pleased at the thought of people in prison!)

But even though their letters come from those being punished for their guilty minds and resultant guilty acts, they have still got much to teach us. This chapter will glance at a few excerpts from letters sent from prison written by a variety of people with different backgrounds and agendas. Obviously they are disguised and 'doctored'. Also the spelling is corrected (I hope!). Please remember that an alarming proportion of prisoners can neither read nor write, and that those who have a degree of literacy include many who struggle greatly even over simple words and sentences.

## Cupboard love?

Not all prisoners' letters are equally inspiring! A few sound like a slightly elongated shopping list, often well decorated by Christian thoughts. See the one below. (The 'diary' which the writer refers to is the Day One diary containing daily Bible texts and attractive scenic photographs. DAYLIGHT Christian Prison Trust helps to organise the distribution of over 170,000 around the prisons on behalf of the generous donor, Day One Prison Ministries. The 'address' referred to in the excerpt is the office address on the diary. For obvious reasons, it is most unwise to give personal addresses in prison.)

'Arthur Carver' writes:

I know you must think what I am doing writing to you, but my solicitor told me to write to you, because I have got a diary from last year which has your address. Anyway what I am trying to say is I'm so ashamed in asking this but could you send me a diary for next year and £20, please, 'cos I have no money in here and my wife can't send in my own. This must sound cheeky to you but God will give it back to you in another way. Please, please help in sending in some money. Thank you. Your brother—etc.'

It is most unwise to send money to prisoners without knowing fully to whom it is going and why. Money can be misused as well as well used in prison. Many requests come by letter and if one was met an avalanche of others would follow. That is not to say that money or a needed gift or Christian book can never be given, through the right procedure and channel, to a known individual.

## A more welcome request

This request from a prisoner in Scotland was willingly met without charge. DAYLIGHT CPT never charges prisoners or chaplaincies for books, booklets, CDs or materials supplied. It is a pleasure and privilege to donate them as God meets the needs. Thousands of the three booklets the inmate refers to (the others are 'How can God accept me?' and 'How can I find God?') are offered personally to inmates as they leave each Sunday service or weekday meeting. More booklets and especially prisoner-friendly tracts are in the pipeline. Around 98% of prisoners who are offered the pieces of literature willingly take them to read or have them read to them— sometimes to relieve the fact that in some prisons inmates can be 'banged up' for over twenty-two hours. Letters like the one quoted below often follow the receipt of those booklets.

I am currently serving an 18 month sentence. I have just finished reading the last of your three booklets entitled 'How can I become a real Christian?' I thoroughly enjoyed reading them and was wondering if you had any other books or booklets that I could read. A fellow prisoner told me that you have an excellent book available 'The Resurrection: the unopened gift'. If possible would it be possible to get a copy sent to me? Please advise me of the cost and I will arrange for a cheque to be sent. I would also appreciate any other books or booklets available.

We hear from women, too, like the one quoted above.

My name is 'Mary Congo' and currently held at the above detention centre awaiting finalisation of my asylum case. I had the pleasure of reading your booklet on 'How can God accept me?' It is really an inspiring little booklet.

Unfortunately on my page 28 there is no address to request for a Bible and humbly ask that if through this address, if possible, my request be directed to the right persons. Any other encouraging material would really be of help here.

Thank you as I eagerly await your response.

Yours etc.

Normally the good-old Gideon Bibles are available in prisons and Immigration Centres, but if an inmate cannot get one, DAYLIGHT sends one with other evangelistic literature.

## A cry from the heart

Can you imagine what it is like to want to know God, and even to 'try to trust Him', and yet have so little understanding and so few Christian contacts to guide you that you remain unsure? We Christians often criticise and take our churches for granted. But just imagine being a seeker with no human being to do for you what Philip did for the seeking Ethiopian eunuch (Acts 8:26–40). Below is a cry from the heart taken from a vulnerable prisoner who was reading the Day One diary each day, but first here is a word of explanation.

A vulnerable prisoner—or VP—is an inmate needing the protection of a separate wing or even a dedicated prison. Most VPs are sex offenders or child abusers, but included in their number are many others. They include, but are not limited to the following: self-harmers and suicidal inmates; those whose physical or mental weakness makes them an easier prey for the prison bullies (always a problem in prison); a gang member who is outnumbered by those belonging to an opposing gang; and imprisoned members of the judiciary, Crown Prosecution Service or police. Some people who are especially vulnerable will receive even stricter surveillance, as seems possibly to be the case cited in this letter. This VP says:

I am currently on protection, which means I don't get much, and I'm always locked up. During this time I was in prison I was bored and needed to change my ways so one day I picked up the Bible and asked Jesus to come into my life, and forgive me for my sins. Since that day I think I am a Christian as I have a different feeling inside me. I also find the Bible a wonderful reading, although some words are hard to read. I was given a Day One diary at Christmas, so I am going to fill it in every day. I already read the daily readings from the Bible.

Is there anything else I can do or say to make my life change and make me a Christian? I have sinned—everybody has. Do I just ask Him to forgive me? I will continue reading the Bible, but look forward to hearing from you.

Thank you very much, etc.

## A high profile young offender's window into being a new Christian 'inside'

Please take it on trust from me that you will have heard about 'Jimmy's' case. He was at a YOI (Young Offenders' Institution) serving time for an offence that was headline news on BBC and ITV. He came to services and meetings and heard the gospel. As a result of that, he asked me to go and spend a pastoral visit with him through the chaplaincy. He also had asked for a copy of *The Bible Panorama*—which explains the whole of the Bible for ordinary people. We had a very personal and detailed talk about Jimmy and about the Lord Jesus Christ who alone could save him and change him. An excerpt from the letter he sent to me later follows:

Thank you for *The Bible Panorama*. You'll be pleased to know that I now read the Bible every day and I kept my promise to read those booklets you handed out. My journey has definitely reached an interesting, if not remarkable, point. I have found myself not only trying to learn more every day but also preaching to others who take an interest. I find myself able to quote passages from the Bible and answer a lot of questions that you would expect of a newcomer. When people ask me do I have any faith I'm able to stand proud and say 'Yes, I am a Christian.' When I am asked do I believe there's a God, I say with no stutter, 'Yes.' Many have asked me why I have put my faith into God and they seem shocked when I say that it has been a life changing experience. One of the staff here told me that 99% of the people who say they have found Christ in prison are simply looking for an excuse.

His insight into the difference between remorse and repentance is also most enlightening. In our humanistic society and legal system, the word 'remorse' is often used in court when a plea of mitigation is being made. Wherever we go, we seek to make clear what the difference is between remorse and repentance—but it is rare to hear that distinction clearly put by an inmate! A man or woman can be sorry about what happened—and especially about getting 'nicked' and about the penalty given—but sorrow for sin that turns that person from sin to Christ is something far deeper. Here is what 'Jimmy' said in the same letter:

To truly become a Christian you have to repent for your ways as well as wanting to change them. Anyone can feel remorseful for their sins. Remorse is simply just feeling sorry for yourself. Anyone can feel bad about what they have done, that doesn't mean they will stop sinning. But what I have experienced is beyond remorse ...

All this was from a young man with no background in the Bible! The work of the Holy Spirit in his life seems apparent.

But now here is the sad part: after writing that letter he was released before I could reply to him. Despite writing to the non-prison address he gave me, I still wait for his reply. Is he going on with Christ? Did he get to a Bible-believing church? I will keep trying to contact him, but one of the sad things about prison work is that often those who seem to be doing well inside can struggle outside. That is why we need concerned Christians to welcome post-release prisoners and get involved with them before they leave. This is one thing that DAYLIGHT is trying to tackle, but the task is huge, hard and costly.

## Sometimes the sentiments are understated

Dear Mr Chrispin,

My name is 'John Andrews' and at this moment in time I am in prison for the fourth time. I was at church today and was moved by what you said in the service. I'd like to thank you for all your hard work and I hope one day I can thank you in person.

God bless,

# Chapter 8

Yours faithfully,

'John Andrews'

My letter to 'John' in reply included the following words:

As you face a New Year please remember that Jesus can forgive and cleanse everything of the past, change our lives now and give us a home in heaven when we die.

I sincerely hope and pray that your trust will be in Him who died for you on the cross.

Please keep in touch.

God bless, etc.

I would love to meet that man soon again on earth, and I would thrill to meet him in heaven. He never did keep in touch. I wonder if his letter was a passing feeling or the start of a new life? I comfort myself by two things: first, God is sovereign and in control; second, lots of people are poor at replying to letters, even outside prison! However, I would so love to see more fruit in clear conversions of prisoners.

## Out for Christmas!

What a joy to receive a letter that started and ended with a looking forward to a different Christmas!

Dear Gerard & Phillippa,

Merry Christmas Both!

My time has come that we can celebrate Christmas together this year. The weeks have gone fast since my homecoming and a lot has been happening. I managed to get myself a job almost straight away ... This will be the first time in our married life that we have gone out on Christmas Day ... Susie is a softy and wants to make my Christmas special this year and we are looking forward to it very much ... Well dear friends this is just a quick catch up letter. Take care of yourselves and we will be in touch after Christmas ...

That might not sound to you to be a very special letter to include in this chapter, but it is. After eight years inside for a crime which I do not believe he committed, and after a serious and only barely unsuccessful suicide attempt, and after his coming to put his trust in Christ as his Saviour which has made him a completely new man, and after his shattered marriage had been put lovingly together again—after all that and a lot more—this was a very special letter from someone who has become a good friend to my dear Phillippa and to me. We treasure it! What a God of mercy and grace we have!

## What price forgiveness?

Sometimes speaking at prison services and meetings puts you in contact with individuals who really open up to you. I never pry into another person's personal circumstances, but often some inmates want to get things off their chest—and off their guilty record before God. Sometimes the discussion carries on by mail. The extract of the letter that follows is most moving and challenging, and it shows what a great responsibility we have in sharing the truth and obligations of God's Word, as well as the privilege of broadcasting its amazing message of forgiveness and restoration.

I have decided to want Jesus Christ in my life, and am prepared to accept the punishment for what I have done. In moments of complete darkness it is good to read the Bible, to give me strength. What I am doing now has left me without my family, instead of carrying on with the deceit and lies which would have been, I am sure, an easy way—but not the right way. Your letters have helped so much to know that it can happen with Jesus in my life. Once again thank you for your work in helping me to find Him.

If you and I had to face years in prison for confessing the sins that we needed to confess in order to come to Christ for pardon and eternal life, would we ever have confessed them? Forgiveness is the free gift of God's generous grace. But it cost the Lord Jesus so much—physical and mental abuse, rejection, false accusation, being forsaken by His friends, death on the cross, separation from His eternal Father, being made sin for us, and taking the eternal judgement of God's wrath for us. A sinner coming to Christ can do nothing to buy what is a free gift, but the need to repent and turn from sins can cost dearly in its consequences afterwards. Would you thank someone for helping you to choose prison?

### Here is one of the boldest excerpts of a letter from prison

The selection of letters chosen from my files has been random and not specially selected. But one of the boldest written excerpts came from a man who had been in prison before and would be again. You might say that he was no stranger to recidivism (re-offending). Here are two sentences taken from what he wrote from a city jail:

Pray for me that I may be able to speak freely here to make known the gospel. I am [a bit like] an ambassador in chains. Pray that I may speak out about it as is my obvious duty.

At a time when the death sentence was very much in existence, the apostle Paul lived under the threat of it day after day. Yet, despite floggings and cruel treatment, he remained resolute and even joyful. Here he writes to the Ephesians from custody in Rome, having just exhorted his readers to live and fight a spiritual warfare like well-equipped Christian soldiers against all the forces of evil. (See Ephesians 6:10–20—the above quote is adapted and shortened from J B Phillips' paraphrase.) Another time when he was in prison in Rome, Paul wrote to the Christians at Philippi. He rejoiced that his chains had given the opportunity for him to identify with and share Christ to all there who knew of his plight. He also was grateful to God that His grace in keeping and blessing him in chains had actually increased the confidence of watching fellow Christians. Against the trend of human fear, God's grace had made them bold to witness, spurred on by his godly and wholehearted example behind bars. (Read Philippians 1:12–18.)

### I was in prison and you came to me—Matthew 25:36

We started by saying that there is a difference between those imprisoned wrongly and those whose crimes have put them there. But do remember that there are backsliding Christians whose downward rebellion results in custodial sentences, and others who come to the Lord in prison, and also a few Christians who are among the wrongly imprisoned minority. Whatever the reason for these men and women entering prison, if they have come to true repentance and restoration and therefore walk with their risen Lord, they each become, in a very real sense, 'an ambassador in chains' for Christ. As such, they must take on the Christian armour that Paul recommended to the Ephesian church. They will certainly need it in the trenches of spiritual warfare in our testing prison system. They also need and should have our prayers and our support. Christians and Christian churches should get to know them well inside prison so they can be encouraged to live for Christ now and be helped to continue to live for Him when they are released. Careful and wise letter writing can be a small part of that.

But how involved is the Christian church in prison and prisoners? Do most Christians see it as an arena of need or as a spectacle to watch from afar? How much of the resources of time, money and effort are channelled into this needy mission field by individual believers and by Christian churches?

Perhaps those are personal questions that should be answered by each of us.

*If you want to see some more correspondence from the other side of the bars, read Appendix 1, 'More from the prison mail bag'. Identities and prison locations are withheld and some necessary editing has taken place.*

# Chapter 8

Philippians 1:

12 But I want you to know, brethren, that the things which happened to me have actually turned out for the furtherance of the gospel, 13 so that it has become evident to the whole palace guard, and to all the rest, that my chains are in Christ; 14 and most of the brethren in the Lord, having become confident by my chains, are much more bold to speak the word without fear. 15 Some indeed preach Christ even from envy and strife, and some also from good will: 16 The former preach Christ from selfish ambition, not sincerely, supposing to add affliction to my chains; 17 but the latter out of love, knowing that I am appointed for the defence of the gospel. 18 What then? Only that in every way, whether in pretence or in truth, Christ is preached; and in this I rejoice, yes, and will rejoice.

# The great escape!

## What some prisoners will try to do to escape from prison

### Saturday morning

'We don't wear a special uniform here,' Mike volunteered, 'so it was dead easy.' I had never heard an escape from prison described as 'dead easy' before! That Saturday morning we had been invited to share the good news of the Saviour from sin with the inmates at his prison. Afterwards we mingled and chatted over a cup of tea or coffee. In the relatively relaxed attitude, Mike opened up about all kinds of things. He even volunteered some details of his crimes—a thing which we never raise in prisons ourselves and do not report outside. With a certain amount of pride he explained how he had escaped from another 'nick'.

'It was a Saturday morning—like today.' Mike was warming to his subject! 'There were two new "screws" on duty—at least I hadn't seen them before. This party of visitors—never found out who they were—came for a guided tour of our "nick". I think there were about twelve of them. They walked around for a bit and then came back to where I was. They were all dressed casual, too. So I joined them! We all walked through the gate when one of the "screws" unlocked it. I even got chatting a bit to one of them—but none of them was posh or stuck up, so I felt OK.'

I asked Mike what happened when he got to the next locked gate. 'Same thing, mate. Just the same thing again!' He grinned triumphantly. 'Getting through the gates wasn't the hardest bit. It was getting past the bloke doing the security checks near the main gate. That worried me to begin with.'

I asked how that had been negotiated. 'Well, in the event that wasn't all that hard, either!' he replied. 'He couldn't easily see everyone from that window—at least not at the same time—and there were enough of us for me to hide behind the others. In any case they all were moving around a bit. The bloke behind the window tried his best to look through and count but he got it a bit wrong. Good job for me! He took each visitor's badge back—you know, the badges that they gave them when they came in—and I just moved past the window when he was looking at the badges. He never even noticed me.'

Someone asked him how long he had stayed out. 'Not very long, mate. They caught me the same day—but it was great fun while it lasted!'

In the friendly chat that followed, the conversation naturally turned to the message shared that morning of how Jesus had carried our sins and punishment on the cross to forgive and save those who would turn from their wrongdoing to Him. I shared with him how he could have a real escape from something far worse than a long custodial sentence, through the risen Son of God who could make him really free. He chatted seriously and happily took a booklet to read about the gospel.

## Can you believe all that you hear?

I have no way of sensibly verifying the truthfulness—or part truthfulness!—of such stories. Exaggeration is not unknown 'inside' prison any more than 'outside' it. But Mike's story did seem to me to be simple enough to be true, and I have since heard from someone I trust and respect of a similar episode taking place elsewhere. But some stories do seem too far-fetched to be true. Take Rocky, for example.

Rocky ended up inside when the authorities decided to round up a number of trouble makers who were posing a threat to them and disturbing society too much. This was before there were 'ASBOs' (Anti-Social Behaviour Orders). In fact, many people believed that the police overreacted and went much too far in imprisoning Rocky. We sometimes read of someone being taken into custody who seemed relatively harmless, or even with a valid point to make (like the old-age pensioner jailed for stating his objection to homosexuality). Such a person may be stubborn (if you oppose him) or resolute (if you support him) but not really a 'bad criminal'. It is true that sometime earlier, Rocky, taking a blade, had assaulted a man in a tense situation where he had not instigated the trouble (there were no charges laid), but he was not really a 'bad person'. That incident was completely out of character and his best friend had put it right for him. True, his brother had lost his life in similar circumstances to those in which Rocky found himself, and Rocky was well known in his neighbourhood with an extremely high profile. But there was no hard evidence of any recent serious or life-threatening criminal behaviour by Rocky. Be that as it may, he found himself inside prison.

His escape story really seems very far-fetched indeed—far more 'stretched' than Mike's relatively credible account of that Saturday morning in his prison. According to Rocky, he was fast asleep and very safely secured. There were, in fact, two extra officers on duty who were detailed to guard him, because of his very high profile. Rocky said that someone he did not know approached him in the night, with a light! A likely story in the middle of what had been effectively a Category A prison. (Category A prisons have the highest level of security.) This unknown person is supposed to have told him to get dressed and then to have led him out of the prison, past two sets of officers. (There are normally at least two significant locking gates in prison before you get near the outer gate.) He said that the big outside gate—made of solid iron—then just opened. According to Rocky, all the security systems were like green traffic lights! No locks, gates, doors or prison officers held him up and no one even noticed that he was escaping! Not even one of his inmates seemed to have realized what was happening. He said he then thought he was dreaming, but afterwards insisted he was not. When he got outside, his mysterious 'deliverer' suddenly disappeared. Rocky later maintained that the severest discipline was administered to those who were guarding him, though no names seem to have been supplied as evidence. Rocky did not escape finally, however. Though the actual evidence has always been hard to tie down precisely, the street talk was that he was cruelly put to a slow and painful death by the authorities.

### Helicopter lifts, or over the wall, or down the fence?

Some prisons have wires stretched over open spaces, and especially over exercise yards. Attached to those wires are big round spheres—like threaded giant footballs. The reason? More than once, a helicopter has flown in to lift out prisoners during exercise time.

It is less rare for men to devise means to get to the outside wall and scale it. When you see the numbers of officers, gates and locks and the high walls topped with razor wire—not to mention the 'electronic beaks' that are placed along the top of many outside prison walls—you wonder how it can ever happen. Yet it has happened from time to time. Actually there are pretty few escapes when you think of the approximately 85,000 men and women incarcerated in the UK's prisons at any one time—and most officers and official visitors are made very security conscious by an increasingly vigilant and attentive security staff. However, one prisoner was escaping over the wall at a southern prison only to be spotted by someone working at the garden centre nearby. Like Mike, he was not out for long—but unlike Mike I do not think he found it 'great fun while it lasted', nor when he was recaptured!

Another prison had layers of extremely high and very strong close mesh wire fencing, again topped generously with razor wire. According to my source of information, volunteered some time after the event (which always has to be a little 'iffy' in prison), during exercise time one inmate drew the attention of the officers by vomiting. While they were understandably trying to help him, another man, who had concealed towels under his top, incredibly scaled the outside wire fence as if he had been travelling horizontally rather than vertically. He then placed the towels over the razor wire, scaled down the other side and dropped—unharmed—onto his feet on the other side of the wire fence. He was then literally now only feet from the officers, but on the other side of the fence. They were able to persuade him of the stupidity of what he had done and that he could not possibly escape, so he agreed to walk around the wire fence to meet them at the front gate. He started to do that, much to their relief. They did not know that the man's colleagues were waiting near the front gate in a fast car with the engine running! He escaped—and I am told also escaped later when stopped by police *en route*—and was only recaptured by chance during a police drugs raid on premises he just happened to be visiting! It seems a pity that such good planning and initiative was reserved for criminal activity. Think what similar application of planning expertise and personal initiative could do for the National Health Service or for one of our leaking water boards!

### ... or even under the van?

But, for me, one of the bravest (or most stupid?) escape attempts involved an illegal immigrant. Every visitor to any prison must notice the angled mirrors on long poles that can be placed under vehicles to ensure there are no passengers underneath. Their very presence—plus the usual diligence of prison officers—means very few would attempt an escape that way. But there is always one! This illegal immigrant decided to chance it and managed to crawl unseen under a parked van within the prison walls and gates. How and to what he held on, I do not know. But hold on he did! That van sped down the motorway at the maximum speed permitted. He must have been both very strong and very desperate—as well as very stupid. Eventually the van slowed down but he still held on in case the journey had not finished. The van slowly started again and then came to a halt and the officers left the vehicle, having securely locked it. When all seemed quiet he got out from underneath—only to find that the van was now locked up inside another prison! If my information is correct, he got back under it and hung on again until the van went out, which it did to park outside the prison walls. But then he was detected in the car park, which was under surveillance.

Just think what a man desperate for freedom and release will risk to try to achieve his liberty. That immigrant could so easily have lost his life. Yet Jesus Christ offers complete liberty from sin's penalty by His death on the cross in our place, and the inner freedom of knowing God's indwelling Spirit as the birthright of everyone who receives Christ to become a child of God. Despite that, men and women refuse to turn from their selfish and sinful lifestyles and to yield to Him as Saviour and Lord. Perhaps if some had been asked to do something dramatic—like holding on to the underneath of a speeding van on a motorway—they might have tried it. The Bible says that forgiveness and eternal life come by God's grace as we trust the Saviour—not by any works that we can do. Perhaps, as guilty sinners, it is that self-humbling that goes against our arrogant human nature and stops us really escaping from death and hell?

## Oh—about Rocky

Finally, did you recognise Rocky's story? Rocky is my nickname for the apostle Peter, of course. You can read the account in Acts 12:1–19. John's brother, James, had been killed by the sword under King Herod's cruel persecution. That pleased the Jews and so Herod took Peter into custody, too—no doubt with a similar fate in mind. God's angel delivered Peter, who was not only incarcerated but also chained and sleeping. The angel led

Peter out of prison, without anyone knowing, before he left him. Peter had really thought that he was seeing a vision and it took him some time to come back to earth and find out that his escape really had happened.

He went to the house of Mary, John Mark's mother, where the local Christians were praying for him! The girl who went to the door when Peter knocked was so thrilled to hear his voice that she went in and told the praying Christians that Peter was there. She unthinkingly left him locked outside—in fact it had been easier for him to get out of prison than into the church prayer meeting! They would not believe her and said it must be his angel! (They did not know then how nearly right they had been—it was his angel who had delivered him.)

Peter told them what had happened. He went elsewhere where Herod's men could not find him. After that he left Judea for Caesarea and stayed there. That is the last we hear of Peter in the Acts of the Apostles but he did write two letters—1 and 2 Peter. Tradition has it that later he was crucified upside down because he did not consider himself to be worthy to die the same death as the Lord Jesus Christ who had saved him and set him free.

## Two reminders

Two reminders come to us from this event. One is that God can save anyone in any circumstances if he, or she, will trust Him and His initiatives of grace in his, or her, life. That is why Christ died and rose again. The second is that when Christians pray, our sovereign God can work amazing answers to prayer. This should encourage those who know Christ to pray for individual people to be set free from sin both inside and outside prison and to trust God to move to His glory in the most unpromising and dark circumstances.

After all, our Saviour is 'The God of our salvation! Our God is the God of salvation; And to God the Lord belong escapes from death' (Psalm 68:20)—and that includes receiving the assurance of eternal heaven instead of the judgement of eternal death.

But the urgent question remains for some: 'How shall we escape, if we neglect so great a salvation; which at the first began to be spoken by the Lord, and was confirmed unto us by them that heard Him?' (Hebrews 2:3).

**NOW READ WHAT THE BIBLE SAYS IN ACTS 12:1–19:**

Acts 12:1–19

1 Now about that time Herod the king stretched out his hand to harass some from the church. 2 Then he killed James the brother of John with the sword. 3 And because he saw that it pleased the Jews, he proceeded further to seize Peter also. Now it was during the Days of Unleavened Bread. 4 So when he had arrested him, he put him in prison, and delivered him to four squads of soldiers to keep him, intending to bring him before the people after Passover.

5 Peter was therefore kept in prison, but constant prayer was offered to God for him by the church. 6 And when Herod was about to bring him out, that night Peter was sleeping, bound with two chains between two soldiers; and the guards before the door were keeping the prison. 7 Now behold, an angel of the Lord stood by him, and a light shone in the prison; and he struck Peter on the side and raised him up, saying, "Arise quickly!" And his chains fell off his hands. 8 Then the angel said to him, "Gird yourself and tie on your sandals"; and so he did. And he said to him, "Put on your garment and follow me." 9 So he went out and followed him, and did not know that what was done by the angel was real, but thought he was seeing a vision. 10 When they were past the first and the second guard posts, they came to the iron gate that leads to the city, which opened to them of its own accord; and they went out and went down one street, and immediately the angel departed from him. 11 And when Peter had come to himself, he said, "Now I know for certain that the Lord has sent His angel, and has delivered me from the hand of Herod and from all the expectation of the Jewish people." 12 So, when he had considered this, he came to the house of Mary, the mother of John whose surname was Mark, where many were gathered together praying. 13 And as Peter knocked at the door of the gate, a girl named Rhoda came to answer. 14 When she recognized Peter's voice, because of her gladness she did not open the gate, but ran in and announced that Peter stood before the gate. 15 But they said to her, "You are beside yourself!" Yet she kept insisting that it was so. So they said, "It is his angel." 16 Now Peter continued knocking; and when they opened the door and saw him, they were astonished. 17 But motioning to them with his hand to keep silent, he declared to them how the Lord had brought him out of the prison. And he said, "Go, tell these things to James and to the brethren." And he departed and went to another place. 18 Then, as soon as it was day, there was no small stir among the soldiers about what had become

of Peter. [19] But when Herod had searched for him and not found him, he examined the guards and commanded that they should be put to death. And he went down from Judea to Caesarea, and stayed there.

# Prison's regulars—or— putting the faces on recidivism

## Prisoners who keep on returning to prison

### The 'in' word—recidivism

If you mention 'recidivism' to someone, you might get at least one of three reactions. Honest Joe will say, 'What's that, then?' Someone whose pride exceeds his ignorance might nod knowingly and hope you drop the subject before his ignorance comes into the open. Yet another might look smug and talk as with great authority. Now and then 'in' words invade our vocabularies afresh—especially when they are government propelled. Perhaps some politicians think we think they are tackling some issue in a meaningful way if they stick an impressive label on it!

For those who still need to know, here is one English dictionary's definition of the word: 'a habitual relapse into crime'. Collins goes on to tell us 'from Latin *recidivus* falling back'. Do you feel enlightened or smug, now? To most ordinary folks the word 're-offending' needs no definition and is very clear, even though my Collins dictionary seems never to have heard of it!

Prisons in the UK are full and close to being overfull. One 'solution' now suggested is to let criminals out sooner! As our increasingly godless society passes legislation that seems at best compromising the once-established moral standards we confessed and in principle held, we see such moral anarchy and disregard for God and the standards of His Word, that it seems nothing can be done to stop more and more people going to prison.

At worst, the reasoning behind some recent laws seems to be verging on 'Christophobia', as though all will be well if we officially reject Jesus and the Bible. For whatever reasons or prejudices, Christianity does not now seem to be given even the same respect and consideration by Parliament as some minority religions receive. When a huge public outcry against the blasphemous and vile anti-Christian 'Jerry Springer—The Opera' produced an unprecedented number of complaints, the British Broadcasting Corporation ignored the complaints and carried on with its highly offensive broadcast. Compare that to the immediate response to initially far fewer complaints which were raised over the alleged and reprehensible 'racial bullying' of an Indian film star (who, admittedly, was gracious and charming) in the murky TV programme 'Big Brother'. Is it surprising that, along with Britain's highest rates of teenage pregnancy and teenage alcohol consumption in Europe, the rise of AIDS assisted by immorality both heterosexually and homosexually, the rash of anti-social behaviour, and the widespread out of control drunken lawlessness and binge drinking in our city centres, re-offending has become a huge problem for all? We have thrown out the godly restraint of keeping Sunday as the Lord's Day, with its emphasis on worship and family time. We give much prime media time to atheists who cloak their anti-God agenda behind mere theories of 'science'. We have promoted greed beyond all known boundaries by making the national lottery respectable and 'normal' and by encouraging the building of new casinos and promoting an unrealistic 'get rich quick—don't work for it' attitude. We have preferred the views of a homosexual minority to the teaching of Jesus and the Bible about family life and bringing up children. This happens while little children have explicit lessons on sex and sexual perversion taught in school, and mothers and fathers are not allowed to know when contraceptives have been given to their children! I used to think Britain had 'gone mad'. I now am sure it has 'gone bad'.

We cannot sow the seeds of godlessness and reap a harvest of goodness. Whether we are MPs sitting in Parliament or ordinary citizens concerned about safety and security in the streets, in the shops, in the schools and in our homes, we all wonder where the wave of crime is taking us and how to stop it. Many inmates we visit inside prison are those we said 'goodbye' to earlier. They have now returned with another crime on their record. Re-offending is a problem that will not go away and cannot be eradicated by yet more legislation, even if that legislation is sometimes appropriate.

## Back into the quagmire
A caring Christian organisation that valiantly tries to help prisoners after

release stated, 'The Government figures give a 70% rate of reconviction for the type of men we work with [sex offenders]'. When the 'Government figures' say that, we may be very sure that it is not less!

'It's hard, Guv,' confided Pete after a gospel meeting in a YOI. 'I get off drugs in here—though sometimes it's even hard in here because we can always get them—and I want to go straight outside. But it's my mates. Just one slip and I'm off again, and coming back in.' Peer pressure, especially related to the two main 'drivers' of crime—alcohol and drugs—is something that young criminals find at times cannot be resisted from their own will power and in their own strength. Many older prisoners who have 'wised out' for a while inside and kept 'clean' from those motivators for self-destruction, also admit that they find it easy to make resolutions inside prison and faithfully go to the programmes on offer to help them, but that they fail quickly after release, when 'the rubber hits the road'. They often slide back into the quagmire. It takes either a strong-willed person or God's grace in Christ to go straight in such a crooked environment with so many temptations and with such a haunting and fragile past. Moreover, a few who have gone straight may still end up inside for reasons beyond their control.

## 'I've been set up.'

I was surprised to see Tim again as he attended our Christian meeting in a Category B prison. He was not a strong Christian, but he did know the Lord. He had been the long-time chapel orderly at another Category B prison where Phillippa and I met him and got to know him well over the years. He was a softly spoken and hesitant man who had shown a rare gentleness in prison and had progressed from Cat B, without problems, to a Cat C prison. That went well because fairly shortly afterwards we encountered him in Cat D custody. That is where prisoners are given greater freedom and privileges and allowed to make town visits and even take outside jobs while still living in the prison. They are closely monitored, of course.

'What are you doing here, Tim?' I asked. 'You were Cat D and heading for release.'

'I've been set up', he whispered. 'I did nothing wrong—honestly. I was out on licence and this geezer at the hostel didn't like my mate and me because he heard we'd both done time. After my mate moved out, he told the police that I threatened him. I never did—you know me.'

I *do* indeed know him very well. His main problem was not violence, but suggestibility. He was so suggestible that some observers cast serious doubt on the safeness of his original conviction. I know no details, but I was told by one normally reliable source that it followed his confession made during an extremely long police interview. (That, of course, need not mean that the police conduct of the interview was in any way irregular.) Two of his friends who were inmates at one prison experimented to see if Tim would own up to something they knew he had not done. After saying he had not done it, they insisted to him that he must have done, because nobody else could have done it. He then confessed, apparently sincerely. They tried to help him by telling him he should not own up just because someone says he is wrong. He really seems to me to be a most unlikely person to threaten anyone. He also is easy prey for false accusations.

'The police believed this geezer, and I am back inside now.' He shrugged his shoulders as his facial expression seemed to say, 'It's just one of those things that had to happen.' Then he added with a warm smile, 'But I still believe in Jesus.' We had no doubt that Tim had trusted the Lord in prison, long before we got to know him.

## Mark and Harry

Mark's eyes were wild looking. 'When I get out, I'm scared that I will kill the "grass" who stitched me up. And I know where to get a shooter.' Hate was in this young man's heart as well as in his eyes. His politeness to me did not mean he was open to the gospel of repentance and faith in Christ, even though he had asked to see someone because he was frightened of what he might do. It was the prison chaplain, who had already spent time with him, who felt that a new face and a different approach might succeed. It did not, I am afraid—at least not my face and not my approach. How inadequate I feel at times like that.

'I have spent twenty-four of my thirty-nine years inside,' said Harry regretfully. 'For years I have learned to live with prison. Now I'm sick to death of it. I want out.' We have had some great one-on-one conversations with him, but he must see the need to own up to his own sin and turn from it to Christ. For a while he appeared very open and softening to the gospel, but he seems to have hardened over the past year. He used to be a regular at our meeting in the prison where he is serving a life sentence, but now he simply arrives for a few minutes and is rather more of a spectator from outside the group. Mind you, he cannot stop making some serious comments and asking some good questions from 'the touchline'. Will he go back inside when his eventual release comes? We believe it all depends on whether he turns from his sin and trusts the Lord Jesus soon. His position is critical.

Just as the most amazing thing about the human body is that there is so much more that does *not* go wrong, similarly, it is surprising that the high rate of re-offending is not higher still. There is so much scope for prisoners to re-offend. Only God's saving and keeping grace, supported by loving fellowship and gentle accountability, is the sure way of avoiding it. Some men and women are strong enough to 'go it alone' to avoid recidivism—just like some non-Christians can stop smoking or keep to a diet—but still they need the only Saviour, the Lord Jesus Christ, to be able to spend eternity in heaven, and to have joy and peace in leading a straight life.

## Al and Jerry

It is always sad to meet repeated offenders, especially when they are young and perhaps starting out on their criminal 'career'. Al, a young man in a Young Offenders' Institution, said wistfully that every major birthday had been spent in custody. His big fear now was that he would spend the rest of his life in prison. You have to be there when that is said to feel the pathos and tragedy of such a situation. It is amazing how some youngsters who we see on our TV screens (and rightly identify as young hooligans whom cause others a lot of harm) seem to be so vulnerable and asking for help when you go to them in prison. If I had not enjoyed a happy and lovingly supportive family, even before I heard the gospel, I could well have ended up where they are now. That does not excuse their wrongdoing, but it does remind you that here are people precious to God—people who could be a blessing to others if they came to know the Lord Jesus.

Jerry's case really stands out above the rest. There was a conspiracy to kill him, for no valid reason, and he received very real threats to kill. (To prove 'threats to kill' in the UK the prosecution must show that a genuine intention to carry out those threats existed.) Like many other prisoners, Jerry was himself a victim of others' crimes and hatred. On at least four separate occasions he experienced different forms of custody. He was no stranger to solitary confinement, or the 'seg' (segregation) as it is known inside. While in prison he was subjected to violence, and was given a shamefully poor diet. He was afforded none of the rights now due by law to every prisoner in our country under the Police and Criminal Evidence Act.

## Jerry's tears

Jerry would often be found in tears. Many 'hard men' admit privately to shedding tears in prison, though it would not be 'macho' to confess to it when others are around. Jerry's tears were different. True, he had suffered much sadness in his life—he failed to achieve what he had set his heart on. Yet his tears were for another reason. You see, Jerry (full name Jeremiah) was a godly man, imprisoned for honouring God. His four major concerns came from the depths of his tender heart.

First, he wept because men refused to accept God's word and take it seriously. He felt deeply the affront to God that men and women did not believe Him or honour Him. When you love someone and others do not believe that person, you feel it personally. That is how Jeremiah felt about his Lord God.

Second, this godly prophet was heartbroken because he knew that unrepentant sinners from among his own people would be judged and suffer. Today, can anyone be a real Christian and be unmoved by the knowledge that 'after death the judgement'? Our friends, neighbours, work colleagues and families have eternity to face—with or without Christ. Can we not find it in our hearts to weep? When I see a room or chapel full of offenders, some of whom are also victims, I wonder how many others have suffered, too. While that 'secondary' suffering should produce real compassion and sympathy in us also, it is as nothing when compared with the painful judgement of a lost and enduring eternity to be faced by those who do not know God.

Third, Jeremiah could see the backslidden and indifferent state of many who did claim to believe in God. The flickering and failing light of their compromised lives did nothing to illuminate their dark surroundings of sin and rebellion. God's requirement of holy living was missing. He knew that, as a result, God was being ignored or ridiculed, those away from God were not being brought to him, and the backsliders also were missing out on God's best for them. That made him weep.

And fourth, in his loneliness, he could see no improvement ahead. At times he battled with depression. He saw very little immediate or short-term 'success' in lives being changed and God being glorified. His own unjust imprisonment and hardships, though very hard, were secondary to him. God's interests came first. Loneliness can be very sad—especially when others should have stood with him for God but did not.

## Jeremiah's heart—and mine

As I look at the lostness and darkness of men, women, youths and even children in our society, can I claim to share Jeremiah's heartfelt concerns? Am I so taken up with living my own life—even my own 'evangelical service' life—that I pass them by carelessly? One Young Life hymn says:

Let me look at the crowd as my Saviour did
Till my eyes with tears grow dim.
Let me look till I pity the wandering sheep
And love them for love of Him.

There can be no burden to reach prisoners and social outcasts unless we first have a burden for the lost, and a concern to be about our Father's business—the business of saving souls by His grace and through the gospel of His Son. Prison shows how hardened and unrepentant attitudes destroy people who are little different from many of us.

## Those four concerns

Do we show Jeremiah's real concern at the neglect, ridicule and scorn for God's Word, the Bible? (See the book of Lamentations, for example chapter 1.) If so, do we seek to redress that by urging lost sinners to heed its saving message, and careless Christians to feed seriously on Scripture day by day? And do we *really* believe in hell? Do we hide behind rightful confidence in God's sovereignty by demonstrating culpable indifference that hell is filling up—and not just with lost prisoners? Paul knew more about God's sovereignty than most people. Yet he said, '… knowing therefore the terror of the Lord, we persuade men' (2 Corinthians 5:11). He declared himself to be 'all things to all men, that I might by all means save some' (1 Corinthians 9:22). If we really believed in a heaven to be gained and a hell to be shunned, perhaps we would care more and do more.

Also how concerned are we in our praying, our encouragement, our chiding, our preaching and our example to motivate other Christians to live flat out for God and the gospel? Does not almost any crowd of soccer supporters put our keenness to shame? Why are we not more enthusiastic in supporting the gospel by living for it and proclaiming it to others? Are we saddened at much of the church's current lack of concern and zeal?

## Love obeys

Finally, are we faithful in proclaiming God's truth even if we are not currently seeing any obvious results from it, and feel lonely in our task? Jeremiah was determined to fulfil his commission whether he was visibly successful or not, and even though he was lonely. Our prime duty is to show that we love our wonderful Saviour and Lord by obeying His command. Love obeys. Obedience causes us to take His word and His gospel to all—in prison or out—whether we are a sole voice or not. As standards fall, we will be more and more isolated, as Jeremiah was—but Jesus promised never to leave us nor forsake us. He is our 'Emmanuel'—God with us.

Perhaps, like Jeremiah, some of us who read this will pay the price in the future, through imprisonment, for proclaiming Christ in an increasingly godless and anti-Christian society. It is far better to be imprisoned for that, than to be incarcerated for doing wrong, like Pete, Tim (perhaps!), Mark, Harry and Al. What a lot we owe to our loving Saviour who has saved us from so much shame and other sin that we could have done! May our lives be a grateful testimony to His saving grace!

Meanwhile there are needy people, including those in prison, who need our Saviour.

**NOW READ WHAT THE BIBLE SAYS IN LAMENTATIONS 1:1–22:**

Lamentations 1:

1 How lonely sits the city That was full of people! How like a widow is she, Who was great among the nations! The princess among the provinces Has become a slave! 2 She weeps bitterly in the night, Her tears are on her cheeks; Among all her lovers She has none to comfort her. All her friends have dealt treacherously with her; They have become her enemies. 3 Judah has gone into captivity, Under affliction and hard servitude; She dwells among the nations, She finds no rest; All her persecutors overtake her in dire straits. 4 The roads to Zion mourn Because no one comes to the set feasts. All her gates are desolate; Her priests sigh, Her virgins are afflicted, And she is in bitterness. 5 Her adversaries have become the master, Her enemies prosper; For the LORD has afflicted her Because of the multitude of her transgressions. Her children have gone into captivity before the enemy. 6 And from the daughter of Zion All her splendor has departed. Her princes have become like deer That find no pasture, That flee without strength Before the pursuer. 7 In the days of her affliction and roaming, Jerusalem remembers all her pleasant things That she had in the days of old. When her people fell into the hand of the enemy, With no one to help her, The adversaries saw her And mocked at her downfall. 8 Jerusalem has sinned gravely, Therefore she has become vile. All who honored her despise her Because they have seen her nakedness; Yes, she sighs and turns away. 9 Her uncleanness is in her skirts; She did not consider her destiny; Therefore her collapse was awesome; She had no comforter. "O LORD, behold my affliction, For the enemy is exalted!" 10 The adversary has spread his hand Over all her pleasant things; For she has seen the nations enter her sanctuary, Those whom You commanded Not to enter Your assembly. 11 All her people sigh, They seek bread; They have given their valuables for food to restore life.

"See, O LORD, and consider, For I am scorned.

12 Is it nothing to you, all you who pass by? Behold and see If there is any sorrow like my sorrow, Which has been brought on me, Which the LORD has inflicted In the day of His fierce anger. 13 From above He has sent fire into my bones, And it overpowered them; He has spread a net for my feet And turned me back; He has made me desolate And faint all the day. 14 The yoke of my transgressions was bound; They were woven together by His hands, And thrust upon my neck. He made my strength fail; The Lord

delivered me into the hands of those whom I am not able to withstand. [15] The Lord has trampled underfoot all my mighty men in my midst; He has called an assembly against me To crush my young men; The Lord trampled as in a winepress The virgin daughter of Judah. [16] For these things I weep; My eye, my eye overflows with water; Because the comforter, who should restore my life, Is far from me. My children are desolate Because the enemy prevailed." [17] Zion spreads out her hands, But no one comforts her; The LORD has commanded concerning Jacob That those around him become his adversaries; Jerusalem has become an unclean thing among them. [18] The LORD is righteous, For I rebelled against His commandment. Hear now, all peoples, And behold my sorrow; My virgins and my young men Have gone into captivity. [19] I called for my lovers, But they deceived me; My priests and my elders Breathed their last in the city, While they sought food To restore their life. [20] See, O LORD, that I am in distress; My soul is troubled; My heart is overturned within me, For I have been very rebellious. Outside the sword bereaves, At home it is like death. [21] They have heard that I sigh, But no one comforts me. All my enemies have heard of my trouble; They are glad that You have done it. Bring on the day You have announced, That they may become like me. [22] Let all their wickedness come before You, And do to them as You have done to me For all my transgressions; For my sighs are many, And my heart is faint."

# Me—in prison? The DAYLIGHT story so far

### Or how to try to get out of prison as often as you go in!

### Shocked congregations?

'I have just come out of prison this morning,' the preacher admitted to a stunned middle class congregation. Some looked shocked and others curious.

He added, 'And I am going back inside again on another matter tomorrow.'

That comment seemed offensive or worrying, based on the furrowed brows and disapproving expressions of some. But worse was to come.

'I have been in and out of prison for the last seven years, but I am unrepentant about it. And it has not made me any better. In fact I am glad to say that I have caused others to go to prison, too.'

That really was going much too far for some of the wide-eyed listeners. How on earth could their church leaders allow this habitual unrepentant jailbird to stand before them to teach them the truths of God's Holy Word, the Bible? For others, however, a slow grin began to appear. Perhaps they could sense that something different was coming!

'Don't worry folks.' The preacher grinned too. 'That is my job. I have the great privilege of going to UK prisons to share with the inmates the good news of a personal Saviour from sin, the Lord Jesus Christ! Through DAYLIGHT Christian Prison Trust, we are trying to mobilise many others—speakers, visitors, churches and teams—to do the same thing. That is why I am here today.'

Relief seemed to spread across his hearers like waves of sunshine when the sun appears from behind successive clouds. He added—'Mind you I was in the Scrubs [Wormwood Scrubs] last week and I am sure I recognise some of you here today!' That brought a laugh. The now relaxing congregation settled to hear about the great need of men and women in custody and the striking opportunities to share with them how God can forgive them and turn them around.

If some of the hearers that evening knew that the preacher really believed that some of them were just as needy, before a holy God who hates sin, as his two morning congregations of 'cons' [convicts], they might have laughed less. A sinner is accepted before God because of personal repentant faith in Christ, not because of being religious or going to church.

## We sometimes have to pinch ourselves!

I was that preacher. I told them that Phillippa and I, and our colleagues who also go to prisons with the gospel, sometimes have to pinch ourselves when we are inside prison taking a service or a meeting, or visiting a prisoner or prison chaplain. Are we in a dream? Are we *really* there? Has God *really* called *us* to share this priceless message with folks we would normally never meet or, frankly, formerly have wanted to meet? Yet, now, I personally feel at least as much at home sharing God's word in prisons as I do at churches, conferences or Christian house parties, though I also love to do that! Some of the inmates have become close friends, and we feel a deep compassion for other prisoners too. We also feel deeply for their many victims. That features clearly in what we say when we share the gospel with the inmates.

I am not proud of my old non-Christian past—nor am I proud of my much more recent Christian past, I should add! The only 'precons' [previous convictions] I have are for speeding. But my life is littered with shameful spiritual and practical 'precons'. God sees hatred in the heart as murder, and indulging in lust in the heart as adultery. I often tell our audiences in custody that when I point my *one* finger at them, I have to answer to God (to whom my thumb points) for the *three* fingers pointing back at me. As Phillippa often stresses, we do not go to prison on the moral high ground, but as hopeless sinners who have been forgiven, cleansed and changed by God's amazing mercy and grace. And even then we very often fail. We continually need His unfailing pardon and help.

## Never been 'nicked'

But I have never been sent to prison for wrongdoing. I have never been 'nicked'. The nearest I got to that was the danger of committing some form of serious assault (then as a sixteen-stone rugby player) if I had found the bloke I looked for who had stolen the girlfriend I had at the time. Happily for him and me, in God's grace, that Saturday night search was unsuccessful. By the next time I came across him, my life had been turned round by Christ's indwelling and changing me. I think he was then more 'pulverised' by my friendly invitation for coffee and a chat about what Christ had done for me than ever he would have been by a left hook! He, at least, was glad I had been converted—so was I!

## Prison ministry was for others, not for me

After coming to Christ, I went to prison a few times as part of my Christian service. I made a number of visits to a young man at Armley Jail, Leeds, who awaited trial and, after his conviction, at HMP Wakefield. I knew him through Leeds Young Life's late Saturday night open-air meetings in a somewhat rowdy and boozy Leeds city centre. Then a law student, I followed his murder trial through the Leeds Crown Court. I even was given (unauthorised!) access to him immediately after his eventual conviction for manslaughter, because the Custody Sergeant recognised me as a member of the United Beach Missions team that had looked after his delighted young daughter on holiday at Skegness the summer before! I also spoke once after a Billy Graham film at Wakefield Prison and two or three times I assisted a godly and warm-hearted lay Pentecostal pastor—Pastor Dearnley of Wrenthorpe Mission—at some of his excellent Bible studies at that Category A prison. But that was all, apart from once preaching for Canoga Park Baptist Church visiting a Californian prison. And it was all a long time ago.

I admired and prayed sometimes for some much-valued members of Above Bar Church, Southampton (where I then lived) who helped regularly at Winchester Prison. I never dreamt that one day I would be going there twice a month to share the gospel! Neither did I foresee the close links we would have with the chaplaincy team or that we would occasionally spend 'one-on-one' time with individual prisoners through pastoral visits. (It helps to be an itinerant pastor with the Fellowship of Independent Evangelical Churches.) But at that time, prison ministry was for others, not for me. I was glad and comfortable about that! Though occasionally I did wonder if, perhaps, one day …

## There is no such thing as a free lunch

Then it happened! I had written a book on the resurrection of the Lord Jesus Christ (*The Resurrection: the unopened gift*) for Day One Publications. Day One's General Secretary, John Roberts, invited Phillippa and me for lunch to discuss my writing another book. In the general table talk, he told us about the regular invitations coming to Day One to send speakers to prison chaplaincy services and meetings. These were triggered by the sending (then) of around 130,000 free Day One diaries to the chaplaincies each year. This figure has now reached over 180,000. His council had set aside money to appoint someone to set up, head up and develop Day One Prison Ministries. He looked at me and asked, 'How would it be if you did that?' The rest is history! There really is no such thing as a 'free lunch'. This one took away all our free time for at least the next eight years!

## The front-line prison ministry begins and develops

We set to work to contact the chaplains in the three different prison authorities in England and Wales, in Scotland, and in Northern Ireland (now comprising just over 160 prisons). We asked them to confirm how many diaries they wanted each year, and also to say if they would like us to make a visit to speak at services and meetings. God's hand was on that. The response was so encouraging that we have never looked back from then.

We also provided through Day One, and still provide free of charge now to the prison chaplaincies through DAYLIGHT Christian Prison Trust, thousands each of three photo-illustrated evangelistic booklets. These booklets—*How can God accept me?*, *How can I find God?* and *How can I become a real Christian?*—are taken by prisoners after meetings. They are read in their cells, where they can be 'banged up' for up to twenty-three hours. They led to many prisoners' letters discussing the gospel and asking questions. Other booklets (which, like those three, are not limited to prisons) are in preparation. So is the production of some shorter and simpler gospel leaflets. They, too, will be offered to the prisoners by DAYLIGHT through the chaplaincies. DAYLIGHT also now donates thousands of copies of an excellent CD on John's gospel—beautifully read and clearly explained—to prison chaplaincies for the inmates. This, again, is without charge. But we never forget the immense good will that our close ongoing association with Day One brings; those Day One diaries are so much appreciated as is Day One's generosity in giving them free of charge, year after year.

Soon it became obvious that this huge prison 'pond' needed more 'fishers'. Accordingly, we began to invite some gifted public communicators of the gospel and teachers of the Bible to join us as voluntary 'PMAs'. To support and accompany them we also asked some winsome and wise personal workers to become 'PMVs' [Prison Ministry Visitors]. Both PMAs and PMVs are honorary appointments. They put in as much time as their commitments allow them. One PMA, Paul Philpott, also on the chaplaincy team at HMP Maidstone, soon became the co-ordinator of the PMAs and PMVs. Currently, DAYLIGHT has around forty PMAs but fewer PMVs. Through our PMAs, we often present the gospel at multiple prisons on the same day. (For example, we cover most of the London prisons each Sunday of Spring Bank Holiday weekend.) They also help DAYLIGHT to spread its wings in new areas and in parts where it is hard for us to reach regularly from our base. Scotland is a recent example of that. They are also urged to take teams with them and, where possible, involve churches.

Whether PMAs, Regional Directors (see below), or ourselves, we all have marvellous opportunities to share the gospel. An average Sunday prison congregation is about seventy prisoners, but that can vary from as few as twenty to two hundred and sixty in two sittings. Often we take more than one service. For example, the vulnerable prisoners usually have their own separate service. We have been involved in as many as four, or even five, services on one Sunday. Weekday meetings can last between thirty and ninety minutes and rarely consist of more than thirty inmates. Officers are usually not present where there are fewer than thirty prisoners.

## A most serious task—but with lighter moments

This chapter will conclude later with how the work launched as Day One Prison Ministries developed, as an independent and dedicated Bible-based prison mission, into DAYLIGHT Christian Prison Trust. But first, let me share some lighter moments associated with this vitally serious task.

Although seeking to win prisoners for Christ and helping them beyond that could not be more urgent, a (controlled!) sense of humour is essential. No outline of prison work would be complete without sharing some lighter moments.

### 'They all say that! Now come on!'

My first return visit to HMP Wakefield was over thirty-five years after my previous one with Pastor Dearnley of Wrenthorpe Mission. It was a very hot day. As I (literally) warmed to preaching the gospel I took my blazer off, revealing my biggest mistake of the day! I had put on my blue and white striped shirt—almost exactly the same as the prison uniform! After sharing the gospel with the prison congregation, still in my shirt, I mingled with the men to chat with them.

The time came for the officers to come and collect the prisoners to go back with them to their respective wings. A and B wings were predictably first. Phillippa and I shook hands with and said goodbye to each outgoing inmate. We offered them our booklets as they left. Then the officer for C wing arrived. It was good for me, as a devoted Yorkshireman, to hear that lovely cultured Yorkshire accent again in volume!

'C Wing! C Wing! Come on C Wing!' he bellowed.

As the next group of men gathered, we shook their hands, said our farewells, and gave them their booklets. Then the officer eyeballed this strange pushy bloke in his blue and white striped shirt, and 'eyeballing' me for (very effective!) emphasis, he bellowed at me, almost as loudly as before, 'I said come on C Wing. Come on then, you!'

'But I am the speaker,' I protested quietly, actually feeling guilty for some strange reason! 'I am here to speak at the service.'

'They all say that,' he snapped back. 'They all say that! Now come on! Come on!'

Happily for me, the combination of Phillippa's bringing me my blazer and the chaplain's vouching for me saved me from still being in Wakefield 'nick' now! I no longer wear my blue and white striped shirt in prisons!

### 'She can be very dangerous!'

At the end of a long trip which had commenced with a very early start from our home to take a service one Christmas in a far away prison, the chaplain (whom I will call 'Fred') kindly offered us a cup of coffee in his office before we started our return trip. The busy Christmas period had made its mark on his office. Seven or eight dirty cups contained the remnants of coffee previously enjoyed—some brown, some now cloudy white and one or two certainly greenish! Phillippa's offer to do the washing up was very readily accepted. While I sat down for a brief rest, the chaplain took her through two locked doors of prison bars. No problem! To my surprise, the chaplain was back alone in a couple of minutes—but no Phillippa. I guessed she had been deposited with the inmates working in the kitchen—you know, where carving knives were probably kept!

'You haven't locked Phillippa in with the prisoners, have you Fred?' I asked directly.

'You're not worried about that are you, Gerard?' came his nonchalant and even cheeky reply!

'Yes, I am concerned,' I replied.

'Why's that?' he asked with apparent ignorance and innocence.

'Well, she can be very dangerous! I hope they are safe!'

We both laughed. After a couple of minutes he went to collect the clean cups—oh, and Phillippa, too! She said she had had a great time with the very respectful and friendly men. 'They were lovely to me,' she beamed! I was glad!

## 'Two life sentences!'

At a large London prison I was questioning Phillippa in front of about a hundred and forty men about her coming to Christ. As I teased her mildly on one point, one inmate (he was not the sharpest knife in the drawer!) blurted out,

''Ere! Are you two married, then?'

I assured him that we were, and he immediately replied in a loud voice, ''Ow long 'ave you been married?'

'Thirty-eight years,' was the then accurate answer I gave.

After a tumultuous round of applause from the inmates, who obviously had doubted if such marital survival was possible, the same man chirped up again,

'Firty-eight years! Firty-eight years! 'Ere—that's two life sentences in'it, eh?'

Uproarious laughter followed, but as it subsided, Phillippa capped his remark with,

'Yes—and no remission!'

More laughter. As that died down I put in my two-penny's worth,

'I am not surprised there is no remission. She has never shown any good behaviour!'

Again there was more laughter. The static thus discharged, we got back to presenting the gospel with much goodwill from the men, who now listened even more intently.

### 'If justice were done, mate ...'

I had met the very solid and very strong-looking cockney before the meeting began. We had some pleasant, and humorous, small talk. Then he got serious and told me that he was being interviewed the next day by the police for something he had not done. He said it was a case of wrong ID and he could easily prove that was so. I listened to him, and then the conversation swung back to the gospel.

At the end of the meeting I went round the circle and prayed for the inmates by name. Some had expressed specific prayer points which, when possible, I included along with a prayer for God's salvation blessing on each one. When I got to my cockney friend I prayed that in his case 'justice would be done'. After my prayer he chimed up: 'I didn't like your prayer at all, Gerard!'

'Why not, Harry?'

'Look mate, I did not do this one—they've got the wrong geezer for sure. But I've done lots more they never nicked me for. If justice were done I'd never get out of this place!' We laughed, but he was serious. I am glad to say that a serious conversation about repentance and faith followed, succeeded by exchanges of letters and visits. But he is not saved yet—and he did get convicted, whether rightly or wrongly in that instance.

### Illegal or unlawful?

John is now with the Lord, having died of cancer. He was released from prison on compassionate grounds, having been an exemplary prisoner. I will not forget his cheerfulness and unfailing sense of humour, even during his last weeks. I first met him in a large northern prison when we had a serious discussion about how he had become a Christian and then how his backsliding had put him back inside. He spoke with a degree of humility about his sin and much gratitude about his Saviour. He came to other services we took in other prisons and we had the privilege of visiting him in his cell.

At the end of our very serious first conversation, he asked me, 'Gerard, you are a criminal lawyer, aren't you?'

'I was, John. I was!' I replied.

'Well, please could you explain to me the difference between illegal and unlawful?' I went into a long and technical explanation which left even me a little confused. At the end of that, this big strong man with an even stronger Lancashire accent added wryly, with a twinkle in his eye,

'Oh, I thought an ill eagle was a sick bird!'

I grunted—he was far too big to insult!

He then went on to say that he had once shared a cell with a barrister who had also been an army officer. He explained that he played Scrabble regularly with this man, and gloated as he recalled his lawyer friend's words to him:

'John, how is it that I am an Oxford graduate, a commissioned officer, and a barrister-at-law and yet I can never beat you at Scrabble?'

'It's not all down to education, Gerard,' John correctly commented.

## If only his earlier attempt had been as unsuccessful!

We visited one prison at the start of the Anglican Advent season. Accordingly, the first of five large candles was to be lit at the service. The others were to be lit on successive weeks, ending with the fifth at Christmas to signify the coming into the world of the Lord Jesus Christ, as the 'Light of the world'.

The chaplain gave a cigarette lighter to an inmate and invited him to light the first candle, which was high up on its stand. The inmate was very short, and needed a chair to stand on. Even then, he could not light that candle. The chaplain suddenly looked very concerned. We thought it was because he was having problems in getting the candle lit. It was not until afterwards that we learned that his dismay was not that at all. It was because he had forgotten that the inmate he had chosen was in prison on a very serious high profile arson charge! I do not know the fine details of that offence but I asked myself what a difference it could have made to that man—and perhaps to others—if only his earlier attempt had been as unsuccessful as that one in the prison chapel!

### 'Mr Chrispin has left his sword in the chapel!'

Phillippa and I were walking back with the Salvation Army lady chaplain to the reception area of a Young Offenders' Institution after having a great time with the lads, explaining the gospel and chatting with them about personal issues. Suddenly I remembered—I had left my Bible in prison again! (I think my Bible has spent more time in custody than Al Capone finally did! I often forget it and have to go back for it.) 'Oh, my Bible!' I said to the Salvation Army lady apologetically. With a lovely understanding grin, she turned around and we retraced our steps through the clanky corridors of locked, barred iron gates and walked past inmates' cells. When we got back to the chapel, we found the Coordinating Chaplain, a lovely Christian man with a keen sense of humour, laughing freely. 'What's the matter?' I asked. He then explained that he had seen my Bible in the chapel and to avoid my having to come back in for it, he had phoned down to the reception to tell them to tell me to hold on until he got it back to me. On duty was an officer whose sense of humour and understanding of illustration should not now be commented on! The chaplain had said to him, in all innocence, but admittedly with a little evangelical jargon,

'Mr Chrispin has left his sword in the chapel!'

'What!' he exclaimed. 'A sword!'

He put the phone down quickly and before the chaplain could say 'knife' (or perhaps 'sword'!), two 'heavies' arrived in appropriate gear to combat and overcome the raving lunatic who had a sword in the chapel! When we got back to the chapel, the position had been laughingly explained and the 'sword' was duly handed back to me. On our way out that night, we did not get the warmest 'Good night' that we have ever had at that prison!

The moral of the story? Don't forget your Bible, Gerard!

## Things you never should say in prison

Here are just three examples of what not to say in prison.

### EXAMPLE ONE—TIME FLIES!

I saw a man in the prison congregation whom I had seen some time before in another prison. 'Hello, mate!' I volunteered publicly. 'Great to see you again! Wow, doesn't time fly?'

'Not quick enough mate!' was his minimal reply. Point taken!

### EXAMPLE TWO—SOMETHING THAT COULD NOT FLY!

Our DAYLIGHT Trustees' Chairman and PMA Coordinator, Paul Philpott, tells of his very first visit to an inmate in his cell. He felt nervous and not at all sure what to say. At that time, the prisoner was allowed to have a caged budgie in his cell. Paul saw in that budgie a point of common focus. Without thinking he looked at the budgie and blurted to the prisoner,

'Look at that budgie. Imagine what it must feel like to be cooped up in there all day long, and never get out!'

Paul says that the man looked at him in cold and utter disbelief and nodded knowingly. He said nothing. Paul has often encouraged people starting Christian prison work, who fear about making mistakes, by stating that if he could survive that 'huge clanger' and still be engaged today in serving the Lord in prison, so can they!

### EXAMPLE THREE—THE CHAPLAIN'S 'HOSPITAL PASS'

A hospital pass is a phrase used in rugby to describe when a fierce tackler is running at speed to demolish the man before him holding the ball. Instead of trying to evade or resist the full speed of a head-on tackle, the man with the ball gently lobs it to another player just a couple of feet away. The tackler simply makes a very slight adjustment and launches himself bodily and horizontally at the poor old static receiver of the ball. He gets flattened and crumpled. That is a hospital pass.

One Sunday, I received such a pass in a prison in Northern Ireland, which housed some convicted terrorists. Perhaps I should add that, before I acted as a criminal defence advocate, I had 'learnt my trade' working for the prosecution. That was a good and thorough training ground.

The prison chapel service had reached the point where I was to be introduced as the preacher by the chaplain. Sometimes I tell the men that I was formerly a criminal lawyer, and even that I conducted both prosecutions and defence. (The men do not mind that—they appreciate and are glad that most of their defence barristers have previously conducted prosecutions as part of their rounded professional on-the-job training.) But this occasion was rather different!

The chaplain said how pleased he was to welcome me to speak, and said some kind things about the prison work in which we are involved. So far, so good! Then he added that I had been the 'Branch Chief Prosecutor for the Crown' in a certain town. I had been a Senior Crown Prosecutor, but that 'promotion' to 'Branch Crown Prosecutor' was just not true! No way! But the men did not know that! They hissed and growled. If looks could have killed, they would all have been facing fresh charges!

I had to preach to them after such an introduction—after taking that hospital pass. I had been immediately branded as the enemy! A number of crippling tackles felt and seemed imminent. I prayed that God would overrule and that He would give me the confidence of these men, so I could share the gospel with them.

I had to think on my feet. After all, I might not be on them much longer!

'Gentlemen, it is correct that I did some prosecution work when I first went into criminal law, but I want you to know that I "repented" of that and turned to defence advocacy.' (I grinned and hoped my poor joke would appeal!) 'In fact, because of what I then did as a defence advocate, some men are not inside now who otherwise might have been.' (That was true— I would fight hard in court for an accused man I was defending if he told me he was not guilty, after I had questioned him fully.)

Happily for me, they laughed—the hospital pass was thankfully negated and the violent tackles avoided—and then they listened eagerly to the gospel. In fact I had a better time chatting with them afterwards, as we had some 'common ground' from which to start. It had been a 'hairy' starting moment, however.

## Back to the serious task of developing a mission to reach prisoners for Christ

After the launch into prisons under Day One Prison Ministries, Paul Philpott, Phillippa and I became more and more convinced that a firmly Bible-based UK mission was needed with a clear doctrinal basis. (Please see it in Appendix 1.) This mission would seek to finance and recruit Regional Directors (RDs) in an endeavour to concentrate its efforts to share the gospel with prisoners across the UK, liaise more closely with chaplaincies, and recruit more PMAs and PMVs. Its other goals would be to produce more appropriate literature and courses, and involve keen traditional evangelical churches (including, but not limited to, those in Day One Publications' niche book market) going into prison with the gospel and thereby helping prisoners both after as well as before their release. Initially, we asked Day One to consider taking on this development. Phillippa and I met with the Day One Council to discuss it. The matter was also complicated because I was nearing the normal Day One 'sell-by date' of sixty-five years of age, and by rights I could have been asked to retire.

## Regional Directors

Key to our thinking was the desire to pray in sufficient resources to appoint RDs on a full-time or part-time basis. Our initial thinking was that ten RDs would mirror the ten regions that the Prison Service had envisaged for its own work and follow-up. Each RD would seek to replicate on a smaller scale in his region what I was seeking to do nationally. Instead of 'my' one hundred and sixty-plus prisons, each RD would be responsible for approximately the nearest accessible sixteen or so prisons. But that would cost a lot of money and we would need RDs who were excellent communicators. They would also need to be able to recruit, organise and motivate Christians, churches, PMAs and PMVs and liaise well with chaplaincy staff.

## 'Cross the Atlantic' so to speak

The three of us felt that, with Day One's valuable help and vision, God had enabled us to get the prison plane successfully off the runway, and we did not now want simply to circle the runway and land it where we started. We wanted to 'cross the Atlantic', metaphorically speaking! We felt very definitely that not only must the work continue, but it must also grow in scope and depth in its gospel influence. The Day One Council were fully appreciative and encouraging in their understanding of this. However, because of other pressures on and priorities of the total Day One work, they very reasonably and understandably felt that this would be a diversification too far for Day One Christian Ministries at that time. They had many financial commitments, including the ongoing financing of providing and shipping the Day One diaries to the prisons, and were understandably concerned about where the money would come from to finance the anticipated vastly expanding prison work. They also had to concentrate their efforts on the continual core work of Day One Christian Ministries.

The Day One Council had always been behind the prison work one hundred percent—and still are—and so we were warmly encouraged to form and develop a new independent trust to achieve our goals. For two years, I would continue to direct Day One Prison Ministries at the same time as I would direct the new trust, and with Day One's blessing run them 'in tandem'. In October 2004, DAYLIGHT Christian Prison Trust came into being, with Paul Philpott as the Chairman of the Trustees. We gathered a tremendous team of referees who are recognised Christian leaders. (See the foot of Appendix 1 for the details.) I was appointed as General Director, assisted by Phillippa on an honorary, but certainly full-time basis. We carried on directing Day One Prison Ministries and the wonderful goodwill that the Day One diaries had generated helped us to get DAYLIGHT launched in a sympathetic environment from prison chaplains.

### Three years on

Three years later, God had built a small but talented and dedicated hands-on Trustee Board, provided a growing number of new PMAs, and prompted some churches and pastors to be involved in their local prisons. As God provides both people and resources, we look to add to the appointment of our first salaried Regional Directors. Dr Nigel Robinson became RD for the Midlands in May 2006 and David Fortune joined us as

RD for London and the south in June 2007. Our burden is to find other RDs as soon as God, in His providence, enables, provides for and directs. For that we need a rare blend of wise patience, a sense of urgency for the task, and the provision of God both with regard to the unique people needed and the resources to employ them. The timing is in His hands. We see the RD's role—as well as sharing the gospel and teaching the Bible in prisons—as a multiplier to encourage and help others to get involved in prisons. This is vital for the work of the gospel.

The great need continues to drive us to meet our vision for RDs as prison missionaries all over the UK. But it is not only in the realm of salaried staff that we seek to advance. We are constantly on the lookout for new PMAs (and supporting PMVs). We thank God for the growing number of PMAs in England, Wales and Scotland.

We also enjoy an amazingly close relationship with Prison Fellowship Northern Ireland (PFNI). We go to speak at services, Bible studies, prison meetings, and church 'deputation' meetings in Northern Ireland and much of the programme is meticulously and warmly facilitated and planned for us by PFNI. Some of the most precious Bible studies of the year are with their ex-offenders who meet together at PFNI headquarters in Belfast.

There is also a kind and gracious team of honorary committed Christian helpers in England to whom we are very indebted for all their cheerful encouragement and good, hard work. Without them, we could not cover anything like the ground that we seek to cover. There are still some prisons in the UK which we have not yet visited, and others where we can only go rarely. We love to have serious ongoing links with all the prisons. Obviously we long to put others in contact with prisons where they can have ongoing contact and influence for the gospel.

We also have some plans about producing and running courses in prisons and the production of certain literature. These have been in our mind from the start, but our time, funds and personnel are limited and, as stated above, we have to blend patience and wisdom with urgency in seeking to cover the necessary ground. As this book is published, serious discussions are being conducted with another well known Bible-believing and gospel-teaching organisation about a formal (and informal!) cooperation to teach the gospel systematically in our prisons.

I anticipate and expect that before long I will retire as DAYLIGHT's General Director. I would love in the time left to me in this role to pass the baton of leadership to my successor. I would dearly like to do that while I am still running the race enthusiastically, and not when I am lying exhausted on the ground! Whatever other Christian work may occupy us in the future, I doubt if Phillippa and I will ever be able to resist investing some time in sharing Christ with prisoners, God willing. The need and the opportunity are so compelling.

## DAYLIGHT's ongoing association with Day One Christian Ministries

From October 2004, when DAYLIGHT was founded, Day One generously continued their early enthusiastic support of the prison work by partly supporting it financially for the first two years of DAYLIGHT's existence. This was in addition to continuing the amazing provision of thousands of Day One diaries (now over 180,000) and Scripture calendars surplus to commercial sales. During that time, I continued to direct Day One Prison Ministries in tandem with DAYLIGHT. From the start of 2007, Day One Prison Ministries have been equally supportive and enthusiastic but, as Day One's other commitments have grown, while the support in prayer and financially for DAYLIGHT has been encouraging, Day One no longer has a 'front line in prison' commitment but generously continues to supply the Day One diaries (and surplus calendars) to the prison chaplaincies, with planning help from DAYLIGHT. You might say that, like any good parent, Day One has helped DAYLIGHT to begin to achieve independence but—as most parents are fully aware!—is still needed now and then to give kind, generous and needed support and advice. Day One Prison Ministries itself needs support to aid the DAYLIGHT work in the prisons by providing all those complimentary diaries. It would be a very sad day for DAYLIGHT's work, and for the cause of the gospel in prisons, if there were not sufficient Day One diaries to give to the chaplains for the prisoners! So much of the goodwill towards both the work and the workers emanates from those little diaries.

Both Day One Prison Ministries and DAYLIGHT appreciate their mutual link and intend it to continue and deepen. DAYLIGHT's new literature states that DAYLIGHT works 'in association with Day One Prison Ministries' and the Director of Day One Christian Ministries will continue to be on the DAYLIGHT Council of Reference.

## ... where such an obvious need is met by such an outstanding opportunity ...

Think of our tremendously accessible and currently open prison mission field which comprises this distinct and well-defined 'people group' of men and women, young and old, in custody. There are over 160 prisons housing approximately 85,000 prisoners in custody on any one day in England and Wales, Scotland and Northern Ireland. If the turnover of prisoners throughout the UK is between four and five times per annum (which is what the Scottish Prison Service web-site said was the rate of Scottish prisoner throughput), that would mean between 340,000 and 425,000 prisoners per year go through the UK prison system. Some say the turnover rate is less than that, but the total is still very high and the need is immense.

Here are people in real need of forgiveness, pardon, change and new life—in fact in desperate need of the Lord Jesus Christ and His gospel. And think what the knock-on effect of a prisoner's genuine conversion can be on his, or her, family and friends. Also, when possible, he will do all he can after conversion to put things as right as he can with those he has harmed. That may be too late and too little, but it will indicate a change of heart and avoid having future victims, both primary and secondary. What a need and what an opportunity are packed in this prime open mission field! I have never seen a work where such an obvious need is met by such an outstanding opportunity to share Christ.

Our prayer is that God will enable DAYLIGHT to deepen spiritually, to expand practically, and to involve other Christians and churches to meet this challenge for the sake of the glory of the Lord Jesus Christ and the salvation of men and women. He alone can give real liberty to the prisoners—now and in eternity.

# Beware! You could easily end up in prison!

## Can you avoid going behind bars?

### '... it could never happen to me ...'

A good friend of ours who is the Coordinating Chaplain at a large southern prison said: 'If you want to make God laugh, tell Him your plans!' He had vowed never to serve under a certain prison Governor with whom he had disagreed openly a number of times on some important issues. After moving from the prison where we first met him, guess where he ended up? That's right—at the next prison to which his former boss had moved. More than that, he went there at the express and pressing invitation of that Governor. That said a lot for both of them.

When my sister, Avril, turned to Christ and began to pray for and witness to her arrogant brother—me!—I remember saying to her, 'It's all right for you, but it could never happen to me.' I came to ask Christ to save me about a year after that!

On the road to Damascus to persecute his hated Christian targets, Paul (then Saul) was met by Jesus Christ when a bright light outshone the sun. Jesus said, 'Saul, Saul, why are you persecuting Me? It is hard for you to kick against the goads' (Acts 26:14). That was an illustration taken from a farmer goading on the oxen that were ploughing the field by jabbing them with a sharp stick, the 'goad'. Sometimes an ox would kick back against the goad. Saul never expected to be converted, much less to witness for Christ, and even far less than that to go to prison himself for that faith in his Saviour. He certainly had no thought that God would use him as an agent through whom the Holy Spirit would reveal a significant proportion of His holy and infallible Word, the Bible. Saul certainly kicked against the goads, as well as kicking against the church in cruel persecution. But before long, he was saved, serving God, and in custody often because he put Christ first. There he actually won prisoners to Christ, as well as being used to write holy Scripture! Saul of Tarsus would never have dreamt that was possible in his worst nightmare!

## So beware!

If witnessing in prison could become a priority to the former arch-enemy of Christianity, you had better beware! I assume that you have not got this far in reading this book if you are totally opposed to the Lord Jesus and His gospel, as was Saul of Tarsus! And if an arrogant sports-mad, pleasure-motivated law student like me could end up passionate about a work I would have gladly avoided at one time, watch out! And remember the comment of our prison chaplain friend!

The amazing thing that many people find about serving Christ in prison is that what started as a spectator sport became a compelling passion.

## Students and Prison Ministry Associates

I think of some faithful and very helpful Oak Hill theological students who often come with us to London prisons. It gladdens my heart to see them get heartily involved in talking to people who are so far removed from their normal life of study. Their homiletics lectures do not, I imagine, explain what to do when a mass punch-up is feared and anticipated, as was the apprehension at one big prison on one Sunday morning! But this is life at ground level. (In fact the punch-up did not materialise—it seems that the preaching of the gospel really had a definite calming influence in prison that morning.) Some of those students really seem to have the prison bug! I hope DAYLIGHT will see much more of them after graduation.

Then I consider some of our gifted and faithful PMAs. Initially one of them, an experienced preacher of the gospel, was not sure if he could take on 'another commitment' to go and preach in prisons on some Sundays. He already went out often to share Christ at church services. (He still does that, by the way, as I do myself.) After he had seen the overwhelming need and the wonderful opportunity to explain the meaning of the cross to an eagerly listening, hugely unchurched, congregation of convicted criminals and remand prisoners, he changed his mind. Why? Because he reckoned that he had reached considerably more outsiders with the gospel on that one visit to prison than in all the churches in which he preached on all the Sunday mornings in the preceding year. Obviously that is *not* to say that we should not minister in other churches or attend our own! It does, however, raise the questions as to whether we can neglect sowing gospel seed in some very fertile ploughed fields, and whether we are in danger of missing reaping souls for Christ in some fields that are 'white unto harvest'. As with all else, balance is needed—but it does not seem to me that we have the balance right yet. This man will happily take more prison opportunities now.

## 'Gobsmacked!'

Nigel Robinson is our first salaried RD, mainly working in Midlands prisons. I remember when, for the first time, we took him with us to a prison near his home just so he could evaluate the opportunity and decide upon his commitment to it. I spoke at two services, each with about eighty men attending. Nigel is always a very interesting person to listen to— whether in public or in private, he is an easy communicator. But on the way home from that prison and for an hour afterwards we could hardly get a word out of him. Whether you like the slang word or not, he really was 'gobsmacked'! He told us afterwards that he was literally in shock at experiencing such a heart-rending need and such a glorious occasion to explain to listening outsiders how they can get right with God. What started as a legitimate spectacle for Nigel has become life changing. He said to me recently, 'Gerard, I am doing now what I always wanted to do and didn't even know it!'

## 'The half has never been told!'

Not everyone is a theological student or a Nigel Robinson. But we are equally thrilled by folks who may not yet have the public gift of communicating the gospel or teaching the Bible, but who just want to come, or pray, or give, or choose any combination of those to help the cause of the gospel in prison. I believe that if you begin to pray, you begin to get involved in all kinds of ways. One young student, on taking his first job, nearly brought me to tears by the amount of sponsorship units he committed to DAYLIGHT, as soon as he began to get paid. Now he has offered to increase it to support DAYLIGHT's sending to prison chaplaincies, to give to inmates, those thousands of excellent complimentary CDs of John's Gospel I mentioned earlier. (John Hawley, one of our PMAs, a long-time Young Life and United Beach Missions friend, and a full-time worker with Open Air Mission, expounds the text simply and clearly, and Pastor Spencer Shaw and Dr Sally Venn read the chapters alternately and beautifully.) That same generous young man came on our team recently one Sunday morning and commented afterwards, 'The half has never been told.' He, too, has the prison bug and wants to come more often.

## Be careful about conferences, too!

Our second RD, this time on a full-time basis, is David Fortune. David had been a pastor for twenty-five years. He had been involved in prisons, and still had the burden inside but had so much to do for the Lord, for the gospel, for the church and for the flock that when circumstances meant he would cease from his prison activities, he never found his way back in. But he came to a John MacArthur UK conference where DAYLIGHT was conducting a prison seminar. At the time it seemed impossible that he could get into prison work full-time, because of a whole range of reasons. Recently he joined DAYLIGHT as the RD for London and the south, after God made a way through those circumstances. David loves people and loved his pastorate, but he is now overwhelmed with the joy and privilege of making Christ known in prisons, and helping others to do so. Beware of conferences!

## 'Our work is brief—its results can be eternal'

The message below came by email from a fine pastor, 'William'. He serves in a small local church. This all started because he contacted me to say that his church wanted to know about the prison work and pray for it. He invited me to speak, which I did after sharing the gospel at his nearest prison, where he now ministers with his team. There are other churches and pastors at various stages of prison involvement. That is not always easy—one immensely gifted and suited pastor has had set-back after set-back in getting in, but we are still praying and trying to get him openings.

I have edited slightly what William wrote:

It was through your leaflet 'Our Work is Brief—Its Results Can Be Eternal' that I was first prompted to consider the possibility of visiting regularly our local prison, HMP Prisonville [real name provided].

Initially, through your ministry, a Sunday service was arranged there as a sort of 'toe in the water' experiment. The services went well (there were two of them), and I could see the potential. Then I got temporary clearance and joined the teams on the wings on several occasions. This was mid-week, and would be our work if we took it on. I found it stimulating, arguing for gospel truth with men who were attending for a whole range of reasons.

The next step was to go to the church, to talk and pray over whether we could make a commitment to this work. We are a small fellowship, already very busy, so this would be a big step, involving a number of our best people. We recognised that this must not be allowed to become our major activity in relation to our duty to build the church and to reach our neighbourhood: the tail must not be allowed to wag the dog. However it was also an opportunity we could not lightly refuse.

We decided to offer the chaplaincy a team capable of running a weekly Bible study on a wing. This would be a team of five men, working on a rota basis, offering a level of continuity, but also allowing for two or even three men to be off at any one time. A team would normally consist of three people.

The offer was accepted, and we applied to gain the security clearance required by the Home Office, which took months. The wheels of bureaucracy moved slowly. We began this September, initially being split up to work alongside experienced visitors, to ease us in, which was helpful. Unfortunately, the evening we go in is not the best for us, (it was changed as we waited clearance and automatically reduced us to four). We've decided to stick with it for the moment and review at the end of the year, when we'll probably change to another night.

## You could pray ...

We are constantly looking for able communicators of the gospel and dedicated personal workers to become PMAs and PMVs. We rejoice whenever a Bible-believing church or fellowship wishes to get involved with inmates, and we love to help if we can. But not everyone can (or should) go into prison to speak, lead a Bible study, run a course, or support those doing so. Not everyone is called to share and help one-on-one with prisoners or correspond with them (which needs to be done very well, very carefully and very thoughtfully). Nor can everyone write a leaflet or booklet or construct or conduct a prison course. (We are still working on that with others, with some exciting possibilities on the horizon, God willing.)

But those who cannot or do not go can pray! DAYLIGHT sends out a three-times-a-year update prayer bulletin and occasional email prayer updates. We desperately need individuals, churches and Christian groups to pray for the work regularly.

## ... or give ...

Many have already greatly encouraged us in the work by giving financially as the Lord prompts and enables. Some give who go. Some give who support in other ways. Some give who pray. We trust the Lord to provide, but have as our policy to make the needs known to Christians and to churches, without harassing anyone. In addition to normal free-will giving, gifts welcomed from Christian trusts (we have not sought finance from those who are not at one with our aims and biblical basis), and 'life-saving legacies', we have a simple sponsorship scheme. Under that scheme, a sponsor donates one or more units—a unit is a pound a month for a year, payable annually, quarterly or monthly. It is simple and helps us to budget. We need very much more in order to appoint the remaining RDs required to present Christ and encourage others to do so in this open and needy mission field. We want to donate many more booklets, tracts, CDs and books, and send as many appropriate people as possible to serve in prison. And remember, please, that Day One also needs support in order to support the prison ministry, as you will have seen in the preceding chapter.

## The men and women in prison and the prison in men and women

Perhaps you could consider praying, giving, or going and encouraging others to consider that too? We are concerned about men and women in prison because the Lord Jesus Christ is concerned about the prison in men and women. I hope you are, too.

www.DaylightCPT.org

# More from the prison mail bag

### Further excerpts from letters—after some editing and with identities withheld

### First, an introductory word ...

The danger of including some excerpts from letters, in addition to those in Chapter 8, is that no one at DAYLIGHT wishes to take the spotlight off the only Person who can meet the needs of sinners anywhere, in or out of prison. That unique Person is, of course, the Lord Jesus Christ. I apologise that it is unavoidable that our work will be quoted in these letters by the inmates who wrote them—because that is why and how we met and corresponded with them. However, the only point we want to make and illustrate is that anyone who is able to preach to, or visit, or write to prisoners, or any combination of those three activities, will find open doors, many heartaches and frustrations, and some blessing in some who do come to Christ, or come back to Him. Please read these excerpts, therefore, with those 'glasses' on—namely what could God do with appropriately gifted servants who will put themselves out to share the gospel with prisoners? A friend of mine once said to me that a wise man learns from his mistakes. That is why we have learned quite a lot! He also said that a wiser man learns from others' mistakes—that is our main qualification for teaching others! But if God can use and bless Phillippa and me, He can certainly do more through many others who, perhaps, have not yet thought about prison ministry.

### Now read some more excerpts from a 'normal' mix from our prison mail bag ...

Sorry it has taken so long to reply. I am no longer on the landings because I had trouble and it all got out of hand so I decided it would be better to be separated from the rest of the inmates. I went to court on 6th August and have to go back on 8th September. Thank you for your letter. I did not receive the Bible reading scheme you sent me. I am not far from finishing the Bible. I have read your book. I thought it was interesting. I hope God can forgive me even though I have sinned against Him. I pray for you and hope that you can start to bring others like me that are in prison or in difficult situations to ask God into their lives. I would like to say a big thank you for helping me to get to know God.

*From a bullied young offender who was seeking to know God. Bullying is a terrible problem even in adult prisons.*

I'm writing today to say thanks for giving our prison an introduction about the Lord God Jesus Christ. I found your speech really interesting. I would like to learn a lot about God and His Son Jesus. If it is possible please could I have a Bible? I would like to be someone that is really close to God and once again thank you for visiting our prison and guiding us in the right path. I would be grateful if you could come back and give us some more encouragement. I would also be grateful for a Day One diary ...

*From another inmate in a Young Offenders' Institution. Once off drugs, some get serious about the gospel.*

I'd been to so many Pentecostal churches but never been touched the way I was in that talk. You were God sent. I don't want to leave the Lord ever again ... I still believe there was a major reason why I attended the chapel the day [of that] powerful and mighty talk ...

*From a prisoner with a clear biblical background. We are saddened to meet those in prison who were Christians when they offended.*

As so many times before over the last two and a half years, despair has turned to confidence in the truth and strength in the knowledge of having done nothing wrong—only for events to start the cycle again. It's been at times of despair that I've most needed to talk to people but then hope comes along again and that need dissipates. So I guess what I am saying is that whenever I've intended to write to you before, positive news has come along, and I've felt that I'll soon be vindicated and the enormity of the nightmare I and my family have been through can be left behind. So I decided to write to you since it now seems the immense emotional rollercoaster of emotions is set to continue for some time yet, and I feel all my strength sapped and spent ...

From a spiritual side, my beliefs have also rocketed from one extreme to another—at times I've been convinced that I have been shown unmistakable evidence of God's intervention. At others, I've felt let down in the worst way. I haven't been a particularly religious person through my life, although I have always believed in some form of spiritual existence … So what I'm saying is I can't make head or tail of my own faith, but would like to at least understand my feelings about this. Knowing that I will have been deeply changed by this experience, it must be a good time to consider this part of my future also … so many questions unanswered—just to talk some of them through would be of great help to me—and you have kindly offered!

*From a man who was headline national news and who, after nearly three years in prison, was acquitted of murder when the judge directed the jury that there was no case to answer. He has become a firm friend, but not yet found his answer.*

Thank you for the words you gave us on Tuesday and Sunday. I am so encouraged by everything. I have come to know Christ here in prison and am enjoying my relationship with Jesus. I don't want to go back to my old ways when I come out of prison. I know that is going to be hard. I ask you to pray for me …

*From a seemingly radiant Christian who, nevertheless, went back from walking with God even before he was released.*

I was privileged to read your little booklet … it made my spirit glad!
*From an inmate in a Scottish prison.*

I have read the prayer on the back page, and I want God to forgive me for all of my sins, as I feel guilty for all the wrong doings that I have done in my life. I'm back in court for sentence on 10th March. I'm scared of going to court. I don't know why but I have tried taking my own life a few times by taking overdoses. Tried hanging myself and cutting up my arms and body to end my life, until I found God waiting for me to come into my life. I don't know any Christian friends, only in jail. Thanks for taking the time to read my letter to you.

*Forwarded to me by an evangelist whose literature I had used in prison. His name was on the booklet.*

Finally, after a lifetime of 'self' living, in spite of a nominal belief in the Lord through a Christian family upbringing, I surrendered my sin-filled life to Him, casting myself on His mercy and forgiveness, having come to the end of justification, excuses, lies and total failure to control my life.

*One of many letters from a man with Christian parents who really seemed to be walking with the Lord in prison. Not long out of prison, he found the battles with sin and self were not left behind the bars that had held him.*

Over the last few weeks I have not been able to read my Bible freely as I would have liked. I have got to have a cellmate on the wing I am on and as you probably know there are people who do not like Christians or those who read the word of God ... I also went back a bit while I was with the other cellmate and was taking drugs while he was here. I know I am weak to temptation but I know Jesus is making me stronger. I know I cannot go back to my home town when I get out because the temptation will be too strong for me there. I do intend to go back there in a few years when I am strong in God and I know nothing will sway me from Him.

*A Welsh prisoner demonstrating how real peer pressure is in prison and how hard it is to deal with. Only God's grace can touch, save, strengthen and keep such men.*

I cannot spell so good but please send me some book that I can learn to know God better.

*From a Jamaican lady prisoner.*

I was in your service on Mothering Sunday. I'm on the mother and baby unit here. I remember you saying that if anyone wanted to write to you, that you would write back. I have read the prayer in the back of the 'How can God accept me?' leaflet. I decided to say the prayer to God with heartfelt meaning. But I am still unsure as to exactly what is expected of me! I would truly like to give my life to God, but I think I need a push in the right direction. Maybe you can help. I hope to hear from you soon ...

*A heart cry from a young mother with a baby writing from prison. Phillippa replied with a gracious 'push' very soon afterwards!*

I thank God every day for people like you and your wife who He called to do prison ministry. It is people like you who come into prisons, but are not part of the prison, that make such a difference to the quality of our lives.

*While we often hear those sentiments sincerely expressed about*

*Christians who go into prison (not just us), one experienced chaplain warned us that the writer was one of the most dangerous prisoners in the UK! You should never relax vigilance or be too gullible in prison.*

Please forgive the delay in my writing back to you after you kindly sent a copy of your book on the Resurrection of Jesus Christ. I went through the book diligently and it was very rewarding. It came at a time when, as a new Christian, I was facing the question 'Is it real?' What a beautiful privilege to be able to say 'Yes!' Know that your book came to me at the right time and it was a pleasure to study … [I] found myself in jail. I was seriously considering ending it all the first week. By God's grace He has allowed me to come closer to Him, so my [imprisonment] has allowed me to come closer to Him, so [it] has turned out to be a real blessing.

*From a letter from an inmate who agreed to look at the evidence for the resurrection of Jesus Christ and consider what the crucified and risen Saviour could do for him.*

I don't know if you can come here on a pastoral visit. The congregations here are very small. It is a little dispiriting when they are so small! I will try the RC church this week which is meant to be a bit better. I have no allegiance to any church: there are so many contradictions and hypocrisy that it is as well in one Christian church as in another. Also I have been having real doubts about the Bible; I have been reading it as if it is real life stories—it 'cannot' be that way. If you do get round to seeing me (I appreciate any visits) I'll explain the reason I am having doubts about the whole belief system … I hope Phillippa is well; please send my best wishes. I look forward to your 'pastoral' visit to help me with some issues! Religious ones!

As always—your friend …

PS Arsenal for the premiership!

PPS If you are about and able to visit, please let me know.

*From another high profile national criminal figure who had been faithfully witnessed to by other Christians, who came along to our meetings, and whom we went to see a number of times. He seems to have lost interest through discouragement but we pray on. We are fond of him.*

All of us here were uplifted with your service and testimony when you came yesterday. While being here on remand for the last three months, I have met with life and Jesus in such fulfilment. I've spent 40 years in the wilderness looking for the wrong answers and then something that you presented is something so simple. Jesus is our Saviour and God is the giver of life and happiness … Thank you for choosing hymn 31, 'Amazing Grace'. It was apt for me … because I've spent so long just going to church, singing the hymns, and falling asleep when the lay reading is going on.

*From a letter received, from the North West, at the time of compiling this appendix.*

I was touched when I listened to John's good news through your CD. In fact God wanted me to have this copy because I was in the prison chapel looking for a book that will calm me down. Suddenly a fellow prisoner came in with two CDs. He gave me a copy—he did not ask me if I wanted one. He just gave it to me. I thanked him for that but I did not have a CD player in my cell. A week later another prisoner came to me straight in my cell and asked me if I would like a CD player. I answered him, 'Yes'. Then he said to me that if I would buy him tobacco for £2·50 then I can have it. I don't smoke but I made the deal with him because I know this is the Lord's doing. Do you know I have been in prison more than three months and no one has ever offered me a CD player to buy. But as soon as I got John's Gospel CD things begin to change. At first I could not sleep properly, but since I listen to this CD, I now sleep like a new born baby who does not have any problems by God's grace. I have two to three months to go out of prison, though I will be deported back to my home country—but no worries because my Lord Jesus Christ has showed me mercy. Even though I am a sinner He will still care for me. He will still care for me. So the good news is about to go back to my own country with the miraculous sign that I have seen.

Thanks and God bless. I look forward to hearing from you soon. Bye.

NB. Please don't mind my writing because I am not a good writer. I was touched to write this letter to let you know what your good works have produced in me.

*From a letter (corrected!) from a foreign criminal due to be deported soon. He had been given a DAYLIGHT CD on John's Gospel—beautifully read and clearly explained by one of our Prison Ministry Associates—and God even provided the CD player!*

To close this brief Appendix of letters from prisoners, here is an email which came from a chaplain at a large, well-known prison. We are struck by the warmth of welcome and friendliness of so many chaplains, who have a hard job to do day after day. Understandably, their theological variety is as wide in prison as outside, but it gladdens my heart to work with the dear Christian brother who wrote this. Please pray for such servants of God!

It was great to have you with us on Sunday. God blessed you and made you a blessing to all of us, staff and inmates alike.

The diaries have arrived today! We are very grateful. People are asking about them all the time. Only today I have given out another copy of *The Bible Panorama* guide to a man called Brian who came here four years ago with a life sentence for murder. He tried to commit suicide and went without food for forty days until he was sectioned and sent to a mental hospital where he has been for the past two years. I have kept visiting him in hospital where they have been absolutely marvellous in their care and treatment. He is now back with us sound and sane—and born again! Gradually over these four years the Spirit of Christ has been working in him and there is no doubt at all that he is now a new creature in Christ. He is remarkably transformed in every way, is on normal location and has a job. Best of all he is reading, reading and reading his Bible. (He was at the service when you came on Sunday.)

Today he said to me 'There's a lot that I don't understand. I need someone to give me a bit of guidance.' I said, 'I've got just the thing for you brother!' and went back to chapel to fetch him a copy of *The Bible Panorama*. He is absolutely delighted! It is just what he needs!

Those dates are all fine. What a privilege that you can give us so much of your precious time and energy! I have put everything in the diary.

# Doctrinal Basis and Official Interpretation

## THE DOCTRINAL BASIS is a belief in:

1 God as the Creator of all men, and the Father of all who believe in the Lord Jesus Christ.

2 The Lord Jesus Christ as the only begotten Son of God, Redeemer of the World, and the one Mediator, through faith in Whom alone we obtain forgiveness of sins.

3 God the Holy Spirit—The Third Person of the Holy Trinity, who regenerates, indwells and transforms every believer, and glorifies the Lord Jesus Christ.

4 The fact of sin, and the necessity of the atonement.

5 The incarnation, sinless life, ministry, death, resurrection, ascension and the personal return of the Lord Jesus Christ.

6 The eternal blessedness of those who are saved, and the eternal punishment of the unsaved.

7 The whole Bible as the inspired, infallible and complete Word of God.

## THE OFFICIAL INTERPRETATION of the Doctrinal Basis is:

Clause 1: (a) God created man in His own image (Genesis 1:26–27; 5:1; 9:6; Psalm 100:3).

(b) There is an essential difference between the relationship of God to the world in general, and to those who believe in the Lord Jesus Christ (John 1:12–13; 1 John 3:1; 5:1,12).

Clause 2: The pre-existence and essential deity of the Lord Jesus Christ (John 1:1–14; John 3:16; Acts 4:12; Romans 3:24; 1 Timothy 2:5–6; Colossians 1:14–18; Acts 13:38–39; Ephesians 1:7; 1 John 4:9–10).

Clause 3: God the Holy Spirit is He Who regenerates, indwells and sanctifies every believer, guiding into all truth, and glorifying the Lord Jesus Christ (John 16:7–14; 3:5–8; 7:39; Romans 8:9,14,16; 2 Thessalonians 2:13; 1 Peter 1:2; John 14:26)

Clause 4: The fact of universal sin (Romans 3:23; 5:12) and the need for reconciliation (Hebrews 9:22). That reconciliation is the work of the Lord Jesus Christ and of Him alone (John 1:29; Romans 3:19–26; Hebrews 9:26–28; 2 Corinthians 5:18–19).

Clause 5: (a) The Lord Jesus Christ is the Incarnate Son of God (Matthew 3:17) born of the virgin Mary (Matthew 1:20–23; Luke 1:35)

(b) His unique revelation and ministry (Hebrews 1:1–3; Luke 19:10).

(c) The substitutionary death (2 Corinthians 5:21) of the Lord Jesus Christ is one of the fundamental truths of the gospel (1 Peter 3:18; Philippians 2:8).

(d) The bodily resurrection of the Lord Jesus Christ was the cardinal point in apostolic testimony (1 Corinthians 15:1–4; Acts 2:29–36; 3:13–15).

(e) The Lord Jesus Christ ascended into heaven from the midst of His disciples and He now sits at the right hand of the throne of God, where He ever lives to make intercession for us (Acts 1:9; Luke 24:50–53; Hebrews 1:3; 10:12; 7:25).

(f) The Lord Jesus Christ will come again bodily and visibly (Acts 1:11; 1 Thessalonians 4:16).

Clause 6: The believer at death is with Christ in heaven. The unbeliever is consciously separated from God for ever (Matthew 25:46; 2 Thessalonians 1:7–9; John 3:36; Romans 5:8–9; Romans 6:23; Daniel 12:2; Revelation 20:15).

Clause 7: The whole Canon of Scripture is fully trustworthy as originally given, and is the unerring revelation of God (2 Timothy 3:16; 1 Corinthians 2:12–14; 2 Peter 1:20–21; 1 Thessalonians 2:13; Galatians 1:6–8; Jude 3; Deuteronomy 4:2; Proverbs 30:5–6; Revelation 22:18–19).

GERARD CRISPIN

ISBN: 978–1–903087–98–5

240 MM X 165 MM HARD COVER WITH DUST JACKET

672 PAGES

This is a unique introduction to and survey of the Bible, giving an overview of each book of the Bible and taking into consideration the message of each verse, without actually being a verse-by-verse commentary. It provides a series of very memorable outlines for each chapter of the Bible. It also includes a succinct but vigorous defence of the Bible and concludes with a number of reading schemes to guide the reader through the Scriptures.

Reader suitability

• Preachers and Bible study leaders, especially those who want to use or perhaps develop the author's outlines in order to enhance their ministries

• Ordinary people who want to get a better understanding of the 'flow' of the Bible, and some help to understand its meaning in context

• People reading through the Bible in their individual and family devotions.

Gerard Chrispin is a lawyer also qualified and experienced in management. He has travelled widely in both the USA and Europe. As well as being an itinerant Pastor and conference speaker he has developed and directs a far-reaching prison evangelism ministry. He has written *The Resurrection: The Unopened Gift; Philippians for Today; Priorities from Prison* and three evangelistic booklets, all published by Day One. He is married with three adult children and four grandchildren.

**Many generations of devout readers of the Scriptures have found in them the words of eternal life. I commend this volume, whose purpose is to lead people of our day to a like precious faith, to all who are prepared to give the Bible an opportunity to speak to them.**
*LORD MACKAY OF CLASHFERN, FORMER LORD CHANCELLOR OF THE UNITED KINGDOM.*

**—I sincerely hope this excellent work gets a wide readership.**
*PROFESSOR MICHAEL A G HAYKIN, PRINCIPAL, TORONTO BAPTIST SEMINARY, CANADA*

—This timely and impressive tome by Gerard Chrispin is a valuable tool to get us all into the Bible and all the Bible into us; how grateful I am for such a practical help now to continue reading through the whole Bible.

*RICHARD CUNNINGHAM, DIRECTOR OF UCCF, UK*

—Gerard Chrispin has assembled helpful overviews of every passage of Scripture, with clear outlines, that will give you a better grasp of Scripture, no matter where you are in your spiritual journey.

*PHIL JOHNSON, EXECUTIVE DIRECTOR OF GRACE TO YOU, CALIFORNIA, USA*

—I am delighted to recommend a resource which draws us back so clearly to reality.

*RICO TICE, ALL SOULS, LANGHAM PLACE, LONDON*

—If we think of the Bible as a range of mountains, Romans is the Himalayan range. In this excellent summary of its powerful message, Gerard Chrispin proves to be a sure-footed guide, leading us up the rugged pathways of truth to the places from which we get such glorious views of God's plan for his people.

*DR JOHN BLANCHARD, AUTHOR AND SPEAKER, UK (ENDORSING NOTES ON ROMANS)*

—The Bible Panorama is going to really open eyes and hearts about the powerful message of this book.

*GEORGE VERWER, FOUNDER OF OPERATION MOBILISATION*

—This panoramic vista by Gerard Crispin will lead you with certainty through the whole Bible from Genesis to Revelation, and lay a sound foundation for a life of growing understanding of the wonderful Word of God.

*REV. GEOFF THOMAS, PASTOR OF ALFRED PLACE BAPTIST CHURCH, WALES*

—I am enthusiastic about this book. If you want to read through the whole Bible, or to look into just a part of it, it is always useful to have the big picture first. This is what Gerard Chrispin gives us, succinctly, attractively, accurately, and in a way that is easy to remember. Many will now study the Scriptures with new zest.

*REV. DR STUART OLYOTT, PASTORAL DIRECTOR EVANGELICAL MOVEMENT OF WALES*

# About Day One:

## Day One's threefold commitment:

- To be faithful to the Bible, God's inerrant, infallible Word;
- To be relevant to our modern generation;
- To be excellent in our publication standards.

*I continue to be thankful for the publications of Day One. They are biblical; they have sound theology; and they are relative to the issues at hand. The material is condensed and manageable while, at the same time, being complete—a challenging balance to find. We are happy in our ministry to make use of these excellent publications.*

**JOHN MACARTHUR, PASTOR-TEACHER, GRACE COMMUNITY CHURCH, CALIFORNIA**

*It is a great encouragement to see Day One making such excellent progress. Their publications are always biblical, accessible and attractively produced, with no compromise on quality. Long may their progress continue and increase!*

**JOHN BLANCHARD, AUTHOR, EVANGELIST AND APOLOGIST**

Visit our website for more information and to request a free catalogue of our books.

**www.dayone.co.uk**